Table of Contents

Departments

2	**Giving Credit Where It's Due** by Randall J. Strossen, Ph.D.	
4	**Letters to the Editor**	
52	**Calendar**	
67	**Iron Filings** by Randall J. Strossen, Ph.D.	
73	**Captains of Crush® Grippers: Who's New**	
127	**The Iron Mine**	

People

28	**Steve Schmidt: Old-time Strongman Today** by Thom Van Vleck

Training

5	**So . . . You Wanna Get BIG?** by Steve Jeck
7	**Unorthodox Exercises** by Bill Starr
32	**Draft Horse Training** by Tim Piper, M.S. and Mike Waller, M.A.
36	**You Are What You *Don't* Eat: Organic Food and the Strength Athlete, Part II** by Gabriel Josiah
40	**Basketball Rebounding for Coordination, Quickness, and Agility** by Col. (Ret.) Joseph H. Wolfenberger
42	**Roadrash: Playing Around with the Push Sled—Part II** by Matt Shatzkin
44	**The Push–Pull of Things** by John Brookfield
47	**Pushing (Back at) 40** by Steve Brylski
62	**Physical Preparedness for PPP—And Anyone in Pursuit of Good Health** by Ken Best
75	**Overtraining: What It Is and How to Avoid It** by Jim Schmitz
81	**The Art and Science of Recovery** by Brian Mangravite
83	**Foundations: The Kettlemill Challenge** by Jon Bruney
85	**Why Systematic Development of Trainees is the Superior Methodology** by Steven Helmicki
88	**Spotlight on Strength and Skill** by Dr. Ken E. Leistner
92	**My Dinnie Stone Quest, or Two Years Within The Brotherhood of Stone** by Roger Davis
103	**Enter the Kettlebell Plus** by Pavel
111	**How to Generate the Greatest Strength at the Lightest Bodyweight** by Steve Justa
124	**Grassroots to Gold Medals: Play Your Role** by Paul Doherty

Contests

14	**2009 IHGF World Highland Games Championships: A Fight to the Finish** by Francis Brebner
53	**105-kg World Record Breakers: The King Has Lost His Crown** by Jyrki Rantanen
99	**2009 Masters' World Championships: Scottish Masters Athletes Gather in the Highlands** by William M. Scruggs, Ph.D.
107	**2009 USAF Unified National Armwrestling Championships: Arkansas to Italy— Who's Going?** by Denise Wattles
115	**Canada World Strength Presents Fortissimus 2009: Building on the Tradition of Louis Cyr** by William Crawford, M.D.

History

57	**Helmsman of Russian Heavy Athletics: Count G. I. Ribeaupierre** by Joseph Svub
113	**German Men of Might: Andreas Maier** by Gherardo Bonini

Aaron Neighbour gives the Braemar stone his all, putting himself in a solid position on the opening event as he went on to win the historic 2009 IHGF World Championships in Edinburgh, Scotland.
Randall J. Strossen photo.

Giving Credit Where It's Due: Laws, Rules, and the Order of Things

For a while, we had an associate minister in our church whose Southern drawl, stories about his grandmother's fried chicken, and engaging manner often forced me to sit on my hands so that I wouldn't break into applause after his sermons. But don't think this was just entertainment because as Pastor Dean would often remind us, "There are laws," and when he looked you in the eye as he said those three words, you knew he wasn't talking about speed limits.

Spiritual, secular or someplace in between, there are laws, things that define the order of the universe, things so powerful that they will sweep away the ignorant or defiant like a paper cup hit by a tidal wave. They have stood since the beginning of time and remain immutable in our Internet world. Scientists strive to uncover and define them in the physical world, and organized religions are engaged in explaining and reinforcing spiritual laws.

When you lift in competition, there are rules, and not being extremely familiar with the rules is a severe disadvantage to coaches and athletes alike. If you lost an attempt at the Olympics because your coach wasn't fully aware of the rules, you might feel as if this blunder—the stuff of nightmares—cost you dearly. On the other hand, a coach who knows the rules like the back of his hand can play them for every advantage his lifter is entitled to.

But why are there rules—and isn't this whole concept anathema to lifters and other strength athletes, groups largely populated by people who prefer individual to team sports, many of whom have little patience for authoritarian structures?

In the world of science, the highest level of order is called laws, where we find such cornerstones of the physical world as the laws which define gravity or Einstein's formula relating mass and energy. Science also uses strict rules to define how research is conducted and its results interpreted. This is done so that we can say whether the result from your lab means that you are on the verge of winning a Nobel prize or that the guy in the next room just turned on his air conditioner, which had a momentary but cataclysmic impact on your data.

In a parallel way, the strength world has some very lawful relationships and it also has rules, with those rules being vital for giving an order to things, things that go beyond the gym owner who doesn't want chalk on his carpet.

Suppose two guys tell you that they squatted 700 pounds, but one used a Monolift; it took three guys at least as big and strong as the Gillingham brothers to get him into his squat suit; an army of spotters swarmed the lifter and the bar; his squat was above parallel; and drug testing was non-existent. The second guy walked it out;

squatted it without a belt, wraps or spotters; was drug tested at the WADA level; and his bottom position was glutes to ankles. Did they both do the same thing? No more than a canoe and a yacht are interchangeable, even though both are boats.

Rules provide the tools for defining what we can do, and thereby they accurately describe what we actually did. And for everyone who doesn't live in the land of smoke and mirrors, rules are far more than a favorite of dictators: by providing a clear-cut way to interpret what people do, they provide a basis for giving credit where it's due.

As ever, train safely, train wisely, train hard.

Randall J. Strossen, Ph.D.
Publisher & Editor-in-chief

It might not be no-no-no, but this lift is good-good-good: Nowhere in the strength world are rules more disheveled than what is found across the various powerlifting federations. It's no accident that the IPF, with the strictest rules, is the gold standard in the sport, and that when someone says "IPF squat," for example, you know all sorts of things about the lift that give it and the athlete the credibility they deserve. Here, Tony Cardello (USA) dunks 390 kg on his way to winning the 125-kg class at the 2007 IPF World Championships.
Randall J. Strossen photo.

MILO

Published by IronMind Enterprises, Inc.

Randall J. Strossen, Ph.D.
Publisher & Editor-in-chief

Elizabeth M. Hammond
Production Editor

Susan Altman
Production Assistant

P.O. Box 1228
Nevada City, CA 95959 USA
www.ironmind.com
Tel: +530-272-3579
Fax: +530-272-3095
E-mail: sales@ironmind.com

MILO is published quarterly: March, June, September & December
Subscription rates for 4 books are:
Softcover: US$79.95/year USA;
US$89.95/year Canada/Mexico;
US$99.95/year all others
On-line:
US$42.95/year all subscribers

Single issues are:
US$20.00 each + $5.00 S&H USA
(US$7.00 S&H Canada/Mexico;
US$13.00 S&H all others)

Copyright ©2009
IronMind Enterprises, Inc.

All rights reserved.
No part of this publication may be reproduced or transmitted in any form or by any means without prior written permission except in the case of brief quotations embodied in articles and reviews.

Design:
Tony Agpoon
Sausalito, CA

Letters to the Editor

Continuing Organic Food Debate

As follow-up to the letter I submitted earlier about organic foods, the article noted here came out today [A.D. Dangour et al., "Nutritional quality of organic foods: a systematic review," *American Journal of Clinical Nutrition* 2009.] It supports the case that organic foods aren't any more nutritious than conventional foods.

Steve Milloy
JunkScience.com
Potomac, MD

Editor's Note: For another point of view, please see Gabriel Josiah's article on organic food on page 36 of this issue.

A New World Record in Pull-ups?

Czech Jan Kares, who was introduced to *MILO* readers in the June 2006 issue [Letters to the Editor, "Passion for Pull-ups," Vol. 14, No. 1] with a record-setting performance in pull-ups, is still going strong. Last year he performed 3050 pull-ups in a time of 6 hours (it should be a new world record). On 13 June 2009, he set another record, doing 979 pull-ups in 1 hour. He said: "My motivation is to overcome myself." His bodyweight was not stated.

Joseph Svub
Ceska Trebova,
Czech Republic

A Brother in Iron

I had just re-read my copy of the June 2009 *MILO* for about the third time. John Christy's article on 1-arm dumbbell benching struck a chord . . . I was shocked when I found his website, www.real-strengthrealmuscle.com and saw that he had unexpectedly passed away in April.

I have read John's articles in *Hardgainer* and *MILO* for years. His unrelenting espousal of progression on basic exercises and microloads for progression has contributed to those two principles playing a major part in my training and the way I train my clients and athletes. My condolences to his family. Although I was never in contact with John, I felt he was a true brother in iron and I will miss his articles.

Randy Long
Garner, NC

Editor's Note: John Christy's publications are still available on his website at www.realstrengthrealmuscle.com, and sales of these items are greatly appreciated by his family.

So . . . You Wanna Get BIG?

Steve Jeck

Author of *The Stone Lifter* and co-author of *Of Stones and Strength*

"All mortal greatness is but disease."
—Herman Melville

"I want to get big . . . but I don't want to get fat."

The preceding words have been uttered in countless weight rooms and gyms, health food store aisles and parking lots, and in basically every setting where people might discuss the reasons and motivations for lifting weights.

I know in the thirty-plus years that I've been lifting weights as an athlete, coach, teacher, and gym manager, I've heard those words or something like them more times than I care to recall.

I, on the other hand, *have never uttered them.*

You see, I've learned in all these years that there are really only two groups of lifters who claim that they want to get big: Those who genuinely do; and those who want to get big . . . *but not fat.*

There is not anything good, healthy, or desirable about getting fat. Although, I am forever and joyfully reminded of the great Alexeyev's words when asked by a reporter if he didn't think his bodyweight was a bit extreme. Big Vasily simply replied, "Muscle carries itself." Amen.

I am not endorsing getting fat for fat's sake. But what I am saying is that anyone who has grabbed that iron and felt something deep in their bones and DNA say, yes, my son . . . this is your destiny!—that person never wastes his time or breath (or anyone else's) by saying something silly like, "I want to get big . . . *but not fat.*"

> THAT PERSON NEVER WASTES HIS TIME OR BREATH (OR ANYONE ELSE'S) BY SAYING SOMETHING SILLY LIKE, "I WANT TO GET BIG . . . BUT NOT FAT."

You see, their course has been set. And they know what everyone who has ever set a goal and accomplished it knows, and that is when your destination is clear enough, and your motivation for getting there strong enough, you simply don't fret about the details.

I set my heart on climbing yonder peak. I can't walk through the countryside without my eyes being drawn to the summit. Even when the mountain is not within physical sight, my mind clearly focuses on the mountaintop and what one must feel to stand atop it, taking in the breathtaking sights, sounds, and sensations. Guess what . . .

I'm getting to the top!

Now, granted, one could make the case that climbing a mountain is certainly not necessary for one's general health and well-being. Why not try a climbing wall or perhaps a Stairmaster machine? And there are most assuredly saner and safer ways to spend one's leisure time. You could always build a *papier-mâché* mountain or frequent a mountain climbing discussion group—as many of the "experts" you'll encounter there have never actually climbed a mountain, you'll fit right in!

No, we are not talking about what normal and rational people do.

Who, really, in their right mind, would ever want to crawl under a squat bar loaded to 150% of their bodyweight and even flirt with doing 20 repetitions; and then three days later, assuming there is anything left of their soul and sinews, throw another 10 lb. on the bar and dare to take the same perilous and psychedelic journey all over again?

> "WHAT'S WITH THESE DRACONIAN DIETS THESE DAYS," HE BEGAN. "WHEN I WAS MOVING ALL THAT IRON, STEVE, I ATE EVERYTHING . . .

By the way, *if* you're generating that kind of horsepower and moving that kind of poundage, you won't have to worry about getting fat! I'll never forget the conversation I had with Marvin Eder late one night after the annual Oldetime Barbell & Strongmen dinner in New Jersey. "What's with these Draconian diets these days," he began. "When I was moving all that iron, Steve, I ate EVERYTHING: pastrami, chocolate cake—it didn't matter. My body was a nuclear furnace, I burned everything I ate!" The mad, old sage had me so fired up by the end of our discussion that it took me an hour and a half to fall asleep.

No, most beginning or misguided lifters are getting the cart before the horse. Instead of focusing on guzzling a gallon of milk or consuming 6,000 calories a day, they should be focusing on the kind of workout that demands that kind of fuel! Believe me, it exists . . . and believe me, if you follow it, you will get big!

What's that?

"But will I get fat in the process?"

O.K., at this point it is time for you to hand this *MILO* to that guy over there in the squat rack, and go buy yourself some *papier-mâché!* M

Unorthodox Exercises

Bill Starr
Author of *The Strongest Shall Survive: Strength Training for Football* and *Defying Gravity*

In the last few months, I have received letters from a couple of my pen-pal trainees requesting that I provide them with some exercises for their routines that are fun to do. I wrote back to them explaining that when strength training is done in a serious manner, fun isn't part of the deal. Sessions can be enjoyable and rewarding, but not fun. Fun is playing volleyball or racquetball, taking a long walk through the park, or visiting the ocean. Working out with weights is, well, work.

What they were really asking for were some ideas on how to make the workouts more interesting by including one or more exercises that give them some motivation. Over the years, while training various types of strength athletes in a wide variety of sports, I've incorporated a few exercises that I consider unorthodox in routines, and many of my athletes have had a good time doing them (actually, not all of them, as several are extremely taxing). I utilize these movements not as entertainment, but to help the athlete improve a weak area on a specific lift.

I am presenting these unorthodox exercises in this article. While you may not be in need of any of these currently, you may find them useful somewhere down the road; or you may know someone who could benefit from using them.

Cleans while kneeling

There are a number of exercises that can be used to help someone improve his clean, either power or full. High pulls, shrugs, hang cleans, and working in the power rack doing isotonic–isometric contractions are all effective. I like and utilize all of these; yet there is another movement that is quite different from those just mentioned and at which lifters find it a challenge to excel: cleans while kneeling. It's a rather simple way to teach an athlete the many small points of finishing the top pull.

The name pretty much describes how it's done. Kneel on the floor, tuck the bar in snug against your thighs and clean it. It's basically a hang clean without having the benefit of your hips and legs to set the bar in motion.

> I UTILIZE THESE MOVEMENTS NOT AS ENTERTAINMENT, BUT TO HELP THE ATHLETE IMPROVE A WEAK AREA ON A SPECIFIC LIFT.

The exercise is effective when worked diligently because it forces you to concentrate on pulling with just your arms, shoulders, and back.

I start a lifter off with 10 lb. on each side of the bar. I keep the weight light until he gets the feel of the movement, which is different from any other form of cleaning. The closest exercise I can think of is upright rows, but in that lift, the bar isn't racked. Your back has to stay very flat during the exercise—if it rounds, you're not going to be in the proper position to give the bar the needed snap at the finish.

This is an excellent way to teach the sequence of the top pull. When the bar is pulled from the floor, if the start and middle are especially strong, the bar will float through the finish from momentum, and the sequence isn't needed—until, that is, the weights get heavy. However, pulling a bar from dead stop at mid-thigh is an entirely different story. The sequence has to be exact; otherwise, the bar will not be pulled high enough for you to rack it.

The lift is done by the deltoids and traps, and the two prime movers of the upper arm, the brachialis and brachioradialis. I realize that the lats and lumbars also play a role, but it's a minor one in comparison with these four groups. Since it's a short-stroke move, you must center your attention on these target groups. The bar must be pulled in a very precise line in order to rack it. You can lean forward or backward just a bit, although not much because you're planted on your knees.

The object of doing this exercise is to teach you the correct line of pull, when to contract your traps, when to bend your arms, and how to position your elbows at the very finish of the movement. Pull the bar upward so that it's extremely close to your torso, keeping your arms straight. Contract your traps and instantly bend your arms—this combination will provide the thrust to drive the bar upward. When you clean from the floor, you have the advantage of climbing high on your toes to help you elevate the bar, but this is not possible with the kneeling cleans. Finally, you must learn to drive your elbows up and out, not back. Once your elbows turn backward, your traps are out of the picture. So, it's bar close, traps, quickly followed by arms, with the elbows shooting up and out, not back.

Five reps work well. As you tire, you will be forced to focus on all the key form points I just mentioned, and the light poundage will allow you to do that. Once you're able to handle the light weights with ease, move on to 25s or 35s. I had a few athletes who were tall with long torsos who were able to use 45-lb. plates, but they were the exceptions. The smaller plates make for a slightly longer pulling motion, and this helps you do the exercise correctly. Only use as much weight as you can to do the lift perfectly. If your form starts to suffer, go back to a lighter poundage. This is really a drill to isolate the top pull and if you're utilizing sloppy technique, it will carry over to the full-range motion of power or full cleans.

Do a complete workout with these, 5 to 8 sets if you like, and the next time you clean, you'll discover how effective they are.

One-hand snatches

To improve the finish for the snatch, either power of full, I have two exercises in my coaching repertoire. The first is one which is familiar to most, while the other is a bit unusual. One-arm or one-hand snatches have been done since the early years of weightlifting. They were often part of the shows put on by the legendary strongmen of the last century: Eugen Sandow, Hans Beck, and Joseph Steinbach. Sandow, in particular, used a lot of dumbbells in his act, and one-hand snatching was part of weightlifting competitions up until the late 1930s. There's nothing new about doing one-hand snatches, except few people actually do them anymore.

I have found one-hand snatches to be most useful in helping an athlete learn how to finish his pull in the snatch. As with the kneeling cleans, snatching a heavy dumbbell requires that you use the exact same sequence that I previously mentioned: traps, arms, bar close, and elbows up. In addition, your deltoids play a much more significant role in snatching a dumbbell than they do when a bar is used and both arms are involved. Even though momentum helps some, it isn't sufficient when the weights get heavy. Your shoulders are responsible for guiding the bar in the proper line and turning it over at the very top.

These will also reveal if there is a disparity in strength between your two arms. Finding this out is always beneficial—you can do something to remedy the problem. Because there is no floating time with a heavy dumbbell and you must control it fore and aft, your deltoids are going to get stronger and that strength will convert directly to power or full snatches with a bar.

It's a very simple exercise to learn and can be done in a small area, like an apartment. This makes them a good exercise to do on a non-training day or when you want to put in some extra work for your shoulders.

Place the dumbbell between your feet on the floor and grip it firmly. You can use straps if you like, but be sure that you have some short enough so you can release the weight if things go south. Don't place your off hand on your thigh to assist you in pulling the bar upward. You won't have this advantage when you use a bar so don't get used to it. Pull the dumbbell off the floor in a controlled manner and then try to pick up speed as it climbs higher. Pay close attention to the sequence: traps, then arms, and extend up on your toes to get a bit of extra height out of your calves. As you turn the dumbbell over to lock it out overhead, dip under it and push up against it at the same time. Don't just catch it—that's a defensive move. When you exert pressure up against it, it's much easier to control it over your head.

Use your free hand, if you wish, to assist in lowering the dumbbell back down to the floor; and then get set and do another rep. Make sure you work both arms equally, and if you find that one arm is considerably weaker than the other, do another couple of sets on the one that is lagging behind.

When you feel comfortable snatching a dumbbell, try doing the same movement with a bar. These are much harder due to the balance factor, but with some practice, most can handle some weight. The key to making these is to grip the bar exactly in the middle; otherwise, the weight will sway to one side or another and if that sway

> SANDOW, IN PARTICULAR, USED A LOT OF DUMBBELLS IN HIS ACT, AND ONE-HAND SNATCHING WAS PART OF WEIGHTLIFTING COMPETITIONS UP UNTIL THE LATE 1930s.

becomes severe, you will not be able to control the bar overhead.

As with the dumbbell snatches, you can dip under the bar and lock it out; however, you don't want to dip too soon. You have to wait until you've completed the pull because, unlike snatching with two arms, there's very little momentum to aid you. Lock out the bar and hold it for a couple of seconds before lowering it back to the floor, using your free hand for assistance. One arm is always going to be stronger than the other, but if this difference is great, note that and spend time making up the disparity.

Snatch grip throws

One-arm snatches could be classified as fun exercises, and I think this next one fits that category as well: snatch grip throws. These are perhaps my favorite when it comes to unorthodox exercises. Throws cannot be done in every weight facility, though, and you'll soon understand why. The exercise consists of throwing a weighted barbell up as high as possible using a wide or snatch grip. This means that 1) the weight room must have a fairly high ceiling, 2) bumper plates need to be available, and 3) it's best to use an older or not-so-perfect Olympic bar. Even though throws are no harder on a bar than missing a snatch, clean, or jerk, there's no sense taking a chance of damaging a good bar when an imperfect one serves the purpose just as well.

Yet all these limitations are not absolute. In garage gyms, I've taken the athlete outside and done these on the grass. And when there are no bumpers, I do the same thing and use metal plates. If there is only one bar, this works too, and the only thing that gets dinged is the grass.

The purpose behind doing these is for the lifter to learn how to fully extend on his snatches. Most lifters honestly believe that they are indeed extending fully, but in many cases they're not. This is especially useful to those Olympic lifters who are extremely fast—they zip under the bar like a shot. Being quick is certainly an asset, but in many cases, it prevents the lifter from fully extending before he moves under the bar. He is able to get away with this until the weights get really heavy; then it becomes a definite detriment.

This happens frequently with young lifters who possess excellent foot speed and flexibility from the beginning. They establish the habit of pulling the weight just so high and then exploding under the bar—a habit that becomes harder to break the longer they have been doing it. Throws can help. Once a lifter learns to do the movement properly, he gets the feel of what he should be doing when he snatches a weight. Learning doesn't come easily, primarily because it takes some balls to hold your ground while you hurl a weighted barbell directly up over your head.

ONE-ARM SNATCHES COULD BE CLASSIFIED AS FUN EXERCISES, AND I THINK THIS NEXT ONE FITS THAT CATEGORY AS WELL: SNATCH GRIP THROWS.

Everyone, for obvious reasons, is apprehensive about snatch grip throws the first time they do them, so they end up throwing the weight way behind them. That doesn't produce the desired results. The bar must be pulled in the exact same line as it is when you're snatching; otherwise, the exercise is fruitless. You must have the confidence that if you do the movement correctly, there will be ample time for you to step out of the way of the descending barbell.

When possible, I have two or three lifters do these at the same time. This creates a competitive atmosphere and they are less prone to bailing out. In order to get the necessary height, all facets of the pull have to be done absolutely perfectly. This means: a strong start off the floor; a powerful middle; and utilizing the before-mentioned sequence of traps, arms, elbows up, and finishing high on your toes. Plus, the bar must be pulled close to your body so that you can give it some extra juice as you throw it up over your head.

You don't need much weight to make this exercise work. Some female lifters I start out with just an Olympic bar until they gain enough confidence to add the bumper plates. I should note that you shouldn't use those small 5- or 10-lb. plates made for beginners—they're far too fragile for this exercise.

The idea is to get a full extension so that as the bar is released from your hands, your body is perfectly vertical and you are up on your toes. Once you get the idea of what you're trying to accomplish, these are rather easy and great fun. When I had my Olympic lifters at Hopkins do these, I posted one of my lifters at the door to signal if any coach or trainer showed up. They would go nuts if they saw an athlete hurling a loaded barbell high over his head and watching it land with a gigantic crash.

> EVERYONE, FOR OBVIOUS REASONS, IS APPREHENSIVE ABOUT SNATCH GRIP THROWS THE FIRST TIME THEY DO THEM, SO THEY END UP THROWING THE WEIGHT WAY BEHIND THEM.

Throws, naturally, were the center of attention in the weight room, which made the participants enjoy the exercise even more. Some became so proficient that the bar would soar upward three or four feet above their heads. A couple athletes became more adventuresome and would catch the bar as it descended.

Obviously, these are done in singles, and I like the athlete to be fully rested before each attempt so that he can put his full effort and attention into the throw. These are great for Olympic lifters, but they're also extremely beneficial to throwers in the field events, especially shot putters and javelin throwers. It teaches them to extend their bodies to the max before putting a final, powerful boost into the shot or javelin.

Standing supports

Supporting heavy poundage is a great way to overload muscles and attachments. After the off-season strength program is over and the athletes have been tested, I set aside one day for overloading the back and another for the entire structure. For the back, I used a short of shrug (it isn't really a shrug since the bar moves only a few inches). The athlete gets inside a power rack, sets the bar at mid-thigh,

> EVEN THOUGH IT'S A SIMPLE, SHORT MOVE, IT TAKES A BIT OF PRACTICE TO BE ABLE TO HANDLE A HALF TON OR MORE.

and then stands up with it and holds it for a few seconds. This is an extremely powerful position. We always ended up taping more weights to the bar because we ran out of room at the end of the bar. We would tape the extra plates close to the inside collars so the lifter could still grip it correctly. The gym record exceeded 1500 lb.

Even though it's a simple, short move, it takes a bit of practice to be able to handle a half ton or more. First and foremost, you must stay rigidly tight—tight to the point of almost cramping, because if any part of your body is the slightest bit relaxed, you will not be able to move the massive weight and hold it. Secondly, your line has to be precise—if it moves a tiny bit forward, the bar will crash back to the pins. The same thing goes if the line is too far back. That will result in your being knocked out of the power rack as the bar thuds down on the pins.

For the relatively lighter weights, I have the lifters do 2 or 3 reps. This helps them prepare their muscles, tendons, and ligaments for the upcoming stress and allows them to find the tight line which will be needed for the big numbers. Once the poundage gets severe, they do only singles. These are done on Fridays so that the athletes have a few days to recover. They are very taxing, not just because of the massive amount of weight being used, but because they require such a high degree of mental concentration that the nervous system is depleted by the time you finish.

Standing supports using an ultra-heavy weight have been around as long as there have been strongmen. It didn't take a Rhodes Scholar to figure out if you wanted to squat big numbers, you damn well better be able to support it easily. It's best to do these in a power rack which provides some space inside it. They're much more difficult in racks with close uprights that allow no margin of error.

This exercise is both a great strength-developing movement and a great learning tool. No one does them well right away—they're just too different from anything else an athlete has done, including taking a max weight out of a rack to squat it. Every facet of the move has to be exact, such as the placement of the bar on your back. If it's even a teeny-tiny bit off, two things will happen: 1) you will not be able to budge the bar off the pins, and 2) if you do break it from the pins, it will instantly crash back down on them.

Head position becomes critical. Look down slightly and the heavy weight will drag you forward and fall backward or slip over your head. Set your eyes upward and the bar will slide back to the pins. Your feet, hips, and spine have to be directly under the bar. If they're not, you will not be able to break the bar off the pins. Even how you grip the bar becomes an important factor when the weights get heavy. You must squeeze the bar tightly and pull it down into your traps so that it is now part of your body. A lazy grip will cause problems right away.

Perhaps the most important of all, you have to plant your feet on the floor and tighten every muscle from your toes to your neck before you try and move the bar off the pins. Most try to punch the bar off the pins, but this always results in a failure. In order to be successful, you need to follow this procedure. Make sure your body mechanics are without flaw, and then think about pushing your feet down through the floor—this will provide you with the necessary solid base. Now bring that energy, generated by pushing down, up through your legs, hips, back, shoulders, and arms. You should almost be trembling as you exert all the power into the bar. Squeeze it off the pins and when you lock it out, continue to focus on staying tight and in an extreme upright position. Never relax even one iota until the bar is set back down on the pins.

Follow the same reps as with the pulling supports, and be sure that the athletes take some days off after doing them. In addition, supports should not be done very often—about three times a year is enough. The lessons learned from doing them and doing them well carries over immediately. All of my athletes who did supports marveled at how light the weight felt on their backs the next time they squatted.

They're certainly not easy, but in my weird way of thinking, they're fun. It's a heady feeling to be able to stand up with and support close to half a ton, which all of my advanced strength athletes were capable of. The first year I taught anyone how to do standing supports, I had only one athlete who was strong enough to handle much weight. I did them with him to demonstrate the form, and we both went over 900 lb. until the "welder man" stepped in and kept the bar from leaving the pins. We did them on a Friday.

The following Monday when I came into the athletic center, a female basketball player came up to me and said in a tone filled with awe and a bit of disbelief, "Coach Starr, someone told me you squatted with 900 lb. on Friday." I replied, "No, it was 925," and kept walking. A smile stayed on my face the rest of the day.

Backing out of a squat rack with a heavy weight is another type of support that is most beneficial to powerlifters, and it has been used with great success by many of the top competitors for years. Determine how far you need to walk out of the rack to be clear of it and where you will stand to do your squats, and then double that length and mark it on the floor. The two things you must have in order to make these productive is a good dose of courage and two very reliable spotters. Baby steps done with care are the rule for these. You must keep pressure up against the bar and maintain your balance or you'll dump your load in a heartbeat.

For these to be of any value, you need to use no less than 200-lb. more than you can squat. More is even better. This exercise not only builds structural strength, it also enhances overall confidence. I was told that Mike Bridges, the great 181-lb. powerlifter, used 1500 lb. on these. After seeing him squat at the 1970 Worlds, I believed he did have the strength to do such a feat.

Try some or all of these not-so-ordinary exercises and see if they bring you results. If nothing else, you'll know how to do them and will be able to teach others the proper technique in the future. And they may bring a surge of joy to your workout, which is always a nice bonus. **M**

> **NEVER RELAX EVEN ONE IOTA UNTIL THE BAR IS SET BACK DOWN ON THE PINS.**

2009 IHGF World Highland Games Championships:
A Fight to the Finish

Francis Brebner

Seven-time caber world champion

The scene was set for what is being called "the greatest Highland Games ever staged," with people making the pilgrimage from all over the world just to be part of this once-in-a-lifetime historical celebration in honor of all things traditional. The 2009 Homecoming was billed as one the biggest and best Highland Games of this century and the last—and it truly was. Set in the majestic location of Edinburgh, Scotland, in the grounds just opposite Holyrood Castle and guarded by the marvelous hill known as Arthur's Seat, it was just breathtaking, indeed.

It was estimated that between eighty and one hundred thousand spectators poured in through the gates to be part of this history-making event. It included the largest gathering of clans ever witnessed, with the best Highland dancers and multi-pipe bands—including the world famous Lonach Highlanders, the last Highland society of

MILO author and fellow strength athlete Roger Davis of Hemel Hempstead (near London), UK, made the trip: "I had a great time soaking up the atmosphere. I had never been to a Highland Games event before and this was a really good display . . . sorry I had to rush off [after the Games], but the view from Arthur's Seat was calling me (I watched the caber toss from up there), and then my plane was calling even louder." Those who have read Roger's articles know that hill walking is a big part of Roger's training, and Roger took the time to climb the not-insignificant hill across the park, capturing the magnificence of the Games venue, which looked like a miniature encampment of King Arthur's court.

Roger Davis photo.

its type in the world—and the Atholl Highlanders (Europe's last remaining legal private army), who proudly led the mass parade along the historic Edinburgh Mile. Over eight thousand people took part in the march alone, and it was truly a sight to behold.

One of the highlights of the homecoming was, of course, the IHGF World Highland Games Championships, which included the world's top athletes from as far as New Zealand, Australia, Holland, Canada, USA, and Scotland. The heavy athletes had a special surprise: a personal visit by His Royal Highness, The Prince of Wales, accompanied by his wife Camilla, Duchess of Cornwall. Shortly after talking with the athletes, Prince Charles officially opened the Games, which made the whole event even more memorable.

Dianne Bennett read a letter sent by the Governor of California, Arnold Schwarzenegger, on the occasion of the Games, wishing the championships and athletes all the best and applauding the Scottish heritage and tradition being kept alive.

Day One

After the Games opened, the athletes got under way with the 22-lb. Braemar stone. Sean Betz, USA, clinched his first win of the championships with a put of 42'. In second place was Australia's Aaron Neighbour, with a put of 40' 7-1/2", and rounding out the top three was New Zealander Pat Hellier, who came in at 39' 9".

The 28-lb. weight-for-distance proved to be a riveting event, as Larry Brock, USA, let fly with a devastating opening throw of 87' 10" to take the early lead. USA's Harrison Bailey III landed in second place in the first round with 83' 7-1/2", and Neighbour took third with 82' 2-1/2". Surprisingly, Betz was in fourth place with an under-par throw of 80' 7-1/2" in one of his best events—this was a sign of pressure beginning to surface.

In the second round Bailey upped his mark to 85' 1". Neighbour produced a fine throw of 87' 1", which was now sharing the same turf patch as Brock, who generated another fine throw of 87' 8". Hans Lolkema (Netherlands) threw his best of 85' 5" to move ahead of Betz, who fouled out on his second-round throw.

The final round saw Brock belt out a throw of 88' 8", and he looked well content with his mark. This, unexpectedly, was not enough as Neighbour marginally snatched his lead with an amazing throw of 88' 10-3/4", with Brock now dropping into second place, and Harrison Bailey in third with 85' 11-1/2". Betz again fouled out with a throw that was clearly well over 90', as it surpassed the marks of both Neighbour and Brock, and you could see on his face the look of dismay as he knew he had lost valuable points in one of his best events early on in the championships.

> . . . YOU COULD SEE ON HIS FACE THE LOOK OF DISMAY AS HE KNEW HE HAD LOST VALUABLE POINTS IN ONE OF HIS BEST EVENTS SO EARLY ON IN THE CHAMPIONSHIPS.

The caber was the third event of the day. At 19' 8" and 130-lb., with the nicest taper, it proved an effortless task for the athletes, with every athlete turning it in the first round. From there on, we decided to bring forth the 22', 150-lb. challenge caber to use as the competition caber. We witnessed only two tosses out of the total three rounds, and one was a very commendable toss by Brock, nailing a perfect 12:00 for the win, for which he received a roaring applause from the spectators that filled the stands. Also credited with an admirable toss—11:15 for second place —was Lolkema, who showed he is a real force to be reckoned with while competing in his first world championships. Neighbour placed third with a best attempt of 85 degrees.

In the 22-lb. hammer, it was Betz—giving his all and fighting back to regain some of the vital points he had lost in the heavy weight-for-distance—who took the early lead with a throw of 110' 2-1/2". Scotland's Craig Sinclair was hot on Betz's heels with a good opener of 110' 2", but both were passed by Brock,

> THE 28-LB. WEIGHT-FOR-DISTANCE PROVED TO BE A RIVETING EVENT, AS LARRY BROCK, USA, LET FLY WITH A DEVASTATING OPENING THROW OF 87' 10" TO TAKE THE EARLY LEAD.

Arthur's Seat, Holyrood Park, provided a gorgeous and imposing backdrop for the competition field.

On center stage: David P. Webster OBE.

Defending champion Sean Betz got off to a strong start, winning the Braemar stone.

© RANDALL J. STROSSEN, PH.D.

Dianne Bennett (l.) read a letter from California Governor Arnold Schwarzenegger applauding the Highland Games World Championships. Dianne and her late husband, Wag, had befriended and aided Arnold when, according to Wag's obituary in *The Times*, they had taken the "unknown Austrian would-be bodybuilder, desperate for a break into fame and fortune," into their home and under their wing—kindnesses that Arnold has always remembered.

All photos by Randall J. Strossen.

Larry Brock nailed second place in the 28-lb. weight for distance.

Harrison Bailey III wings the 28-lb. weight for distance.

Piping isn't just for men.

Camilla, Duchess of Cornwall, greets David Webster.

The unequalled grandeur of Scottish pipe bands charged the air.

Exuding royalty, Prince Charles, Prince of Wales graciously mixed with the athletes, and his address included poetry by Sir Alexander Gray and Sir Walter Scott.

Hans Llokema, one of only two of the competitors who could turn the caber, launches the big stick.

California was well represented at these championships: with his son Ryan (l.), that's Steve Conway (r.), head referee and known worldwide for his many contributions as the longstanding athletic director for the Caledonian Club of San Francisco's Games at Pleasanton.

The inseparable team of David Webster (l.) and Francis Brebner (r.) kept things well-greased down on the field.

Sean Betz, on the caber, goes along for the ride.

Bill Crawford, M.D. took part in the strongman events that were interspersed with the Highland Games World Championships.

MILO author Roger Davis (l.) chats with production editor Elizabeth Hammond. Besides enjoying the contest and taking some photos, Roger made his exit via the summit of Arthur's Seat, taking full advantage of the opportunity for a nice hill walk along with some photography and spectating.

Laine Snook (l.), who is on IronMind's short list of the world's top grip men, chats with Scottish strongman star Jamie Barr.

With a feather in his visor, Larry Brock warms up for the hammer

Along with the crowds ringing the competition field, a steady stream of hikers headed along the trail for an invigorating walk and a breathtaking view.

A tug-of-war enlivened the day, but challengers (l.) were no match for the know-how and precision work of Team Scotland (r.)

Pat Hellier on the Open Stone, where his strong throws netted him second place.

who let fly with a throw of 112' 10-1/2". In the second round, Betz moved up a gear and belted out 113' 10-1/2" to take the lead over Brock; Sinclair also improved, throwing 112' 6-1/2" and landing firmly in third position.

The final round saw a surprise recovery throw from Neighbour, who crafted a personal best of 111' 2" to move up to fourth position. Neither Sinclair nor Brock advanced with their last throws, but they held on to third and second places respectively. On his final throw, Betz upped his lead with a captivating effort of 117' 1-1/2".

Overall points after Day One:

1.	Aaron Neighbour (AUS)	10
2.	Larry Brock (USA)	11
3.	Sean Betz (USA)	13
4.	Greg Hadley (CAN)	19
5.	Harrison Bailey III (USA)	20
6.	Hans Lolkema (NLD)	21
7.	Pat Hellier (NZD)	23
8.	Craig Sinclair (SCO)	27

Day Two

A light rain could not dampen the spirits of the heavy athletes. The second day of competition got off to a fast-paced start in the 16-lb. open stone in the first round, with Neighbour confidently blasting out a leading put of 53' 4". Hellier was in second place with 51' and Betz was in third with 50' 8-3/4".

In the second round, Neighbour kept up his flowing standard of fine throws by putting up yet another, this time at 53' 5-1/2", with Hellier giving his all with a very dynamic put of 53' 2", which nearly matched the big Australian. Betz was still fighting hard—and still holding onto third spot with an improved mark of 51' 11-1/2".

The final round could not have been more exciting as the top three in this event slugged it out all the way. In the end, the order remained the same: Neighbour sealed the win with an improved throw of 54' 2"; Hellier came in second with 53' 2", and Betz took the third spot with 51' 11-1/2".

Going into the 56-lb. weight-for-distance, the weather started to clear up, and with that, the Games arena began to fill up again with many thousands of spectators.

Brock led the field all the way, with the winning throw of 44' 4-1/2", with Bailey pulling out a clutch throw of 43' 6" for second place over Neighbour, who placed third with 41' 11-1/2".

With only two events left in the championships, the points were tight between the top three: Neighbour led the field with 14 points, Brock followed in second with 17, and Betz was in third with 21. Both Betz and Brock had some work ahead of them to make up crucial ground and would have to dig deep.

> THE FINAL ROUND COULD NOT HAVE BEEN MORE EXCITING AS THE TOP THREE IN THIS EVENT SLUGGED IT OUT ALL THE WAY.

The 16-lb. hammer captured the intensity. In the first round Betz opened with a throw of 130' 9", which was surpassed by Sinclair at 130' 11-1/2", and then by Brock with 131' 1-3/4". In the second round Betz cranked things up a notch and uncorked a throw of 137' 4-1/2". Sinclair also improved with a distance of 135' 1/2"; but for Brock, it was pure pain written all over his face as he released the hammer—a badly swollen ankle was affecting his release as he put all his bodyweight on it, and he could only manage a distance of 128' 1-3/4".

The pressure of the last round was in full effect, with Betz fouling out. The only athlete to improve was Greg Hadley (Canada), with a throw of 130' 1/4" that slid him into fourth place. Sinclair held on to second with 135' 1/2", Brock was in third with 131' 1-3/4", and Betz came out the victor with 137' 4-1/2", clawing back for some vital points.

At the closing stage of the competition, the overall points were tallied up and there was a tie between Brock and Neighbour at 20 points, and Betz had 23. It was now all on the last event—and you could see by the looks on their faces that emotions were running high. Brock, Neighbour, and Betz all tried to keep their cool as they paced about, quietly composing their thoughts and getting their minds set.

> **BOTH BETZ AND BROCK HAD SOME WORK AHEAD OF THEM TO MAKE UP CRUCIAL GROUND AND WOULD HAVE TO DIG DEEP.**

The 56-lb. weight-over-bar was the deciding event to see who would be crowned the 2009 world champion. The opening height was set at 13', with all competitors clearing the bar. The bar was next being raised to 14' and all cleared it on the first round except for Bailey and Hellier, but they were successful on their second attempts.

With the bar now at 15', Lolkema, Betz, and Neighbour cleared it; but it was a shocking disaster for Brock, which resulted in his waving goodbye to his chances of winning yet another world title that he had come so close capturing. Sinclair, Bailey, Hellier, and Hadley also were defeated by this height.

With only three athletes left in the event, the bar was now set at 15' 3", and only Betz and Neighbour prevailed. Finally, the bar was set at 15' 9", which only Neighbour cleared for the win, and he claimed his title of IHGF world champion of 2009.

The final event of the day was the challenge caber (22' long and weighing 150-lb.) and it was a non-scoring event. Only three athletes were able to turn this caber, with Hellier tossing an 11:45 for the win. Lolkema came in second place with 11:15, and Hadley turned the big stick for third place with 11:00.

> **WITH ONLY THREE ATHLETES LEFT IN THE EVENT, THE BAR WAS NOW SET AT 15' 3", AND ONLY BETZ AND NEIGHBOUR PREVAILED.**

2009 IHGF World Championships – Final Points

1.	Aaron Neighbour (AUS)	21
2.	Larry Brock (USA)	24
3.	Sean Betz (USA)	27
4.	Greg Hadley (CAN)	38.5
5.	Harrison Bailey (USA)	39.5
6.	Hans Lolkema (NLD)	45
7.	Pat Hellier (NZD)	45.5
8.	Craig Sinclair (SCO)	50.5

Talking with the newly crowned title-holder Aaron Neighbour, I asked him how he felt now that he was IHGF world champion. Aaron replied, "I am very happy to win the IHGF Worlds, and it makes the win that much more special knowing that it included the highest caliber of athletes assembled from around the world. It makes me very happy, indeed.

"I take my hat off to all the athletes—they really are a great group of guys, and it was one hard-fought competition all the way. It all came down to the very last event for the title, and I must say that I was feeling a little bit stressed, but I have been in this position before in athletics and I was just trying to keep myself together and not blow it.

"I was a little disappointed with my 16-lb. hammer, which I felt I could have done better with, but other than that, all my throwing went well over the course of the championships."

Asking Neighbour what it meant winning the IHGF World Championships, he said, "I was actually selected to compete in this year's World Track and Field Championships in Berlin, which I passed on so I could just concentrate and train harder for the IHGF World Championships.

"In track and field you have three throws and you're done, but in the Highland Games you have seven events and you can fight your way back to win; although, if you mess up bad on one event it could also be over for you."

Reflecting on the Games for myself, this was an amazing event, from its location in Edinburgh to the whole setup of the Games in Holyrood Park. The thousands of spectators who crowded the Games' field is something which I have never seen in all my past days of competing in Scotland. It was a sight to behold, indeed, and gave me a feeling of how it had been in bygone days, before the likes of TV, when Games in Scotland would attract sixty to eighty thousand spectators and more at some of the larger Games. It was a magnificent sight, and all the athletes agreed that this was the best Games ever staged and a memorable sensation that captured the heart and spirit of all things traditional.

It truly was a history-making event that will be remembered by all who made the journey there to watch or to participate in the 2009 Homecoming. M

> THE THOUSANDS OF SPECTATORS WHO CROWDED THE GAMES' FIELD IS SOMETHING WHICH I HAVE NEVER SEEN IN ALL MY PAST DAYS OF COMPETING IN SCOTLAND.

Steve Schmidt:
Old-time Strongman Today
Thom Van Vleck

Steve Schmidt is a weightlifter and strongman who hails from rural Missouri. His career has spanned four decades, and despite his amazing accomplishments, he has garnered little of the recognition he deserves—mainly because he is modest and laid-back about what he does. Steve is one of the best short-steel benders in the world as well as a premier professional strongman in the mold of John Brookfield and Dennis Rogers. What makes him special are his teeth-lifting and pulling feats and how he uses his teeth to bend anything imaginable. Steve is now in his mid-fifties and his journey has been long and twisted, like the steel he leaves in his wake.

Steve began lifting in 1977. He is a fifth-generation cattleman who has always trained alone in a home gym that is as much of a throwback as they come. When he competes, he represents Clark's Gym out of Columbia, Missouri, but in reality, Clark's is a hundred miles from his farm. His career in the strength world has spanned powerlifting, odd lifting and now strongman performances. Steve told me that as he has reached goals in one area of the strength world, he has felt the need to move on to new challenges to keep his motivation high. As a result, he has achieved success in several areas.

I first met Steve Schmidt in 1986 at a small meet at the prison in Moberly, Missouri. At that time, he was a powerlifter from Leslie, Missouri, and I had read his name numerous times in Bill Clark's weightlifting newsletter. Bill used to put on a lot of prison meets to give the incarcerated lifters a chance to lift against outside lifters. I was a young lifter and was in the same weight class as Steve. He was a good lifter and a good sport, and he made a positive impression on me. After that, I made note when I saw his name in the newsletter as he plied his trade as a powerlifter throughout

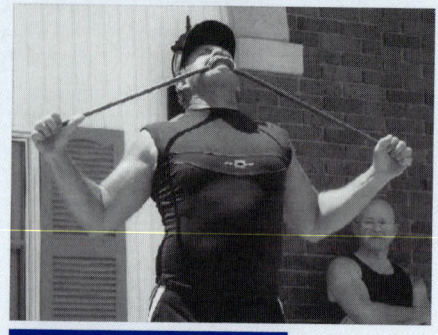

Steve Schmidt bending a steel bar with his teeth.

> STEVE IS NOW IN HIS MID-FIFTIES AND HIS JOURNEY HAS BEEN LONG AND TWISTED, LIKE THE STEEL HE LEAVES IN HIS WAKE.

1. Steve doing a hip lift.

2. Steve working on his 8,000,000-lb. back lift marathon.

3. Steve back lifting 3,050 lb. at the Dino Gym in Holland, Kansas.

4. Steve's "chicken coop" gym.

5. Steve lifting 390 lb. with his teeth.

Photos courtesy of Al Myers.

the 1980s. It would be many more years before our paths crossed again.

Steve was first introduced to the odd lifts in 1981. The odd lifts are a collection of old-time strongman events and some newer, unorthodox lifts kept alive by Ed Zercher Sr., an old-time strongman who started in the 1920s. Bill Clark had taken over this interest in 1959 when he started a strength-related newsletter that would span 50 years and become the longest-running one on record. Steve had found out about Bill through an old edition of Peary Rader's *Iron Man* magazine, and he began competing in Bill's odd-lift meets as an adjunct to his powerlifting career. However, he soon found he had a real aptitude for what were called the "heavy lifts," and as his career progressed into the 1990s, he began to powerlift less and heavy lift more.

The heavy lifts were made famous by Warren Lincoln Travis. These lifts were characterized by extremely heavy weights lifted in very limited ranges of motion, often done for extreme numbers of reps. One is the back lift, which many may recall Paul Anderson doing in his performances. Steve does it on a special apparatus designed for the lift, where the weight is loaded on what amounts to a table; Steve then crawls under the table and uses his legs and arms to push up just an inch or so.

Another is the harness lift, which involves wearing a heavy harness that straps to a special bar that can hold thousands of pounds. The lifter straddles the bar and lifts the weight, again just an inch or so off the floor. Steve is a 14-time heavy lift national champion of the United States All-round Weightlifting Association (USAWA). He has accomplished a 3,515-lb. harness lift and a 3,050-lb. back lift, both USAWA records. Maybe more amazing, in an effort to exceed one of Warren Lincoln Travis's greatest feats and break a USAWA record held by Howard Prechtel for over 20 years, Steve did 7,253 repetitions with 1,115 lb. in the back lift in less than 3 hours. Yes, that's 7,253 reps for a total weight lifted of 8,087,095 lb.! Steve's prowess on the heavy lifts has allowed him to garner three USAWA All-Round National Championships. These events are always decided on total pounds, and when a heavy lift is included, Steve makes up a lot of ground quickly!

Perhaps more amazing is Steve's ability to use his teeth in his lifting and his strongman performances. Steve has done a teeth-lift of 390 lb. with his hands behind his back. Steve bites into a special "bit" that is chained to a pin on a plate-loaded vertical bar, which he then lifts a few inches off the floor. His abilities in teeth-lifting naturally led to bending with his teeth, something that Dennis Rogers marveled at when they performed together at the 2006 Association of Oldtime Barbell and Strongmen (AOBS) dinner in New Jersey. Dennis is known for his unusual feats of strength that often defy common sense and self preservation, and even Dennis said he would not try Steve's feats involving teeth-lifting or teeth-bending.

It was around this time that Steve and I crossed paths again at a USAWA meet. Steve was well into his professional strongman career by this time. He said he first got into steel bending after watching an early World's Strongest Man contest in which the contestants bent steel bars of increasing circumference and decreasing length. He said he went out and bought a bunch of steel of the same size and began bending it. He enjoyed it and found that he had a knack for it. It was only a matter of time before he started bending with his teeth.

> STEVE'S GYM IS AN OLD CHICKEN COOP WITH A DIRT FLOOR.

Steve's gym is an old chicken coop with a dirt floor. There is no electricity and no door. Steve explained, "If I put a door on it, I couldn't see because there's no lights." Much of Steve's equipment is homemade, and the old nesting bins are now filled with short steel, wrenches, horseshoes, and other bending supplies. Some of his stuff is outside and stays there year round. To keep from loading thousands of pounds for every heavy-lift workout, he told me that he warms up with 2,000 lb. on the harness lift and the back lift, keeping that weight on his homemade apparatus at all times.

How Steve got into doing strongman performances was as pragmatic as his lifting career. Through his heavy-lift accomplishments, he was invited to do exhibitions but found it difficult to find enough weight locally to do a back lift. He said, "One time I emptied out the local gym and still didn't have enough weight." Plus, there's the issue of the average person understanding a lift like

> ... AND EVEN DENNIS SAID HE WOULD NOT TRY STEVE'S FEATS INVOLVING TEETH-LIFTING OR TEETH-BENDING.

> "WHAT A DISGRACE IT IS FOR A MAN TO GROW OLD WITHOUT EVER SEEING THE BEAUTY AND STRENGTH OF WHICH HIS BODY IS CAPABLE."

that. Steve decided to start doing his steel bending at exhibitions. He began to add things like wrenches and horseshoes, having some heavy-duty special horseshoes made for his shows by a local Amish blacksmith. Steve told me that it was important to him not to cheat. This meant being drug-free and using legitimate tools, horseshoes, and steel.

Steve told me that when he was a kid, he had two goals, "I wanted to be a farmer and a strongman." He has achieved both with great success—but with much hardship. Steve explained that he lives in a very rural area, and there are no local gyms and nobody else lifts weights. Since he rarely views the Internet or networks with other strongmen, he learned much of his trade on his own and by trial and error. He did all this while running a fifth-generation family farm.

As Steve developed his abilities, the teeth-pulling became a central part of his show. He began to hook his bit on to just about anything he thought he could lift or pull. In the process, he noticed that most of the folks watched the horseshoe, wrench, and nail bending with interest, but when it came to the teeth-pulling, they jumped for a front row seat. Thus, Steve began to pull an assortment of things—really, anything with wheels would get the "Strongman Steve" treatment. He set a world record at the Harvest Festival in Knox, Indiana, in 2008 by pulling nine pick-up trucks, all chained together, with his teeth. The total weight was 56,000 lb. Later this year he is going to attempt to break that record with a pull of 60,000 lb. To date, Steve has pulled all kinds of vehicles, and even trains. The one thing he is still lacking on his resume is a plane. Steve said, "I want to pull a cargo plane, around 50,000 lb."—with his teeth, of course.

Steve has traveled all across the Midwest, entertaining at local events. He only asks to have his expenses covered and when he ends up with extra money, he donates it to the local Humane Society. Steve told me, "This is never something that I wanted to make a living at." Steve lifts and performs for the sheer joy of it. On his gym wall is a quote from Socrates, "What a disgrace it is for a man to grow old without ever seeing the beauty and strength of which his body is capable." In my opinion, Steve has lived up to this quote and continues its practice.

Finally, all Steve's accomplishments have been achieved without the use of any performance-enhancing drugs. Steve is very adamant that his longevity in the sport can be attributed to this fact. Steve told me he'd rather be strong for a lifetime than have any accolades that steroids could bring him in the short term. His 32-year strength career is proof and he continues to improve as he nears his fifty-fourth birthday.

My favorite quote from Steve is, "As long as somebody wants to see me do it, I'll do it. Heck, I'll probably do it when nobody wants to see me do it." I think people will want to see what Steve does for a long time to come.

Draft Horse Training

Tim Piper, M.S. and Mike Waller, M.A.

Anyone who has ever taken the time to watch a draft horse or mule work can quickly understand the sheer brute force these beasts can create. They are large and powerful animals that take on any task before them—or behind them, as the case may be—without flinching. These animals were born for work, and many athletes in strength sports could benefit from training methods that mimic those of the draft horse. After discussing my ideas with Mike Waller and getting his advice, I set out to train like a draft horse. He does think I am a little crazy but he is by no means any different—he is just jealous that he did not think of it first! After many attempts and training days, we decided to share our program with *MILO* readers in hopes that it might inspire others to give it a try.

> As I experimented with pulling the logs, I began to realize that the workhorses and mules make it look entirely too easy.

It was about one year ago, after thinning out some of my pasture, that I developed the idea of working like a draft horse as a method of building stamina, strength, and overall physical conditioning. I had cut down about 50 white pine trees averaging 10-15 ft. in height. I figured I would lash them together with some rope or chain, throw the rope over my shoulder or attach it to a pulling harness, and then start marching. I had little comprehension of just how hard this type of workout would become as it quickly brought me to exhaustion and resulted in days of muscle soreness. Yes, this training was a very grueling—yet fun—workout.

As I experimented with pulling the logs, I began to realize that the workhorses and mules make it look entirely too easy. I first attempted to pull just one log behind me as a warm-up, thinking it would be very easy. Even though I had already chopped the limbs off the trees, I was shocked at how the logs dug into the ground and tried their best to re-root in the earth. Next I attempted to pull three large logs and found out quickly that my mere 190 lb. of bodyweight and tired legs could NOT make this look easy. I dug my boots into the ground, leaned forward, and used all the might I could muster just to pull those three logs about 50 yards to their final destination as part of a trellis I was making. The final eight or so logs I moved in groups of two until I had somewhat recovered, and finished up with a final pull of three more big logs.

> THE FARM ANIMALS JUST IGNORED ME AS I LAY THERE HUFFING AND PUFFING.

That was it. I was spent and actually lay in the yard for a good 15 minutes just to recover. By this time my wife had gone inside, as she was through capturing the pictures for MILO; however, upon seeing me lying in the yard, she wasn't sure if I was resting or if I had suffered the big one! The farm animals just ignored me as I lay there huffing and puffing. Since that day I have pulled logs for another such trellis, with equal difficulty. This training has made me come to really love this type of work, and I believe it is very effective and definitely develops the "old-man strength" we have previously discussed in MILO ["Old Man Strength, or Muscles Don't Know Their Age," MILO, March 2006, Vol. 13, No. 4].

The inherent risks with draft horse training lie in the very heart of what makes it so beneficial. First and foremost, it can be very intense if you push yourself hard while training. Second, it will develop that old-man strength because it does not simulate pulling logs like some piece of gym apparatus. Rather, it is an example of a highly integrated training method that involves total-body muscular work, requires strength from each and every part of your body from your toes to your fingertips, and engages your cardiovascular system in a way that is quite similar to sprint training. If you have the ability, you can even make these exercises into a true cardio workout as long as you can sustain the work for five or more minutes at a time. This is no easy task. Third, the very fact that it relies on and develops your old-man strength makes it a risky endeavor. Most strong older men got that way because they used their bodies in what we now are referring to as functional movements that carry their own inherent risks due to the many skills they employ all at once.

The exercises

The exercises used for draft horse-style training are described below. Feel free to develop your own variations if you have other equipment or ideas, using common sense and safe training.

Words of caution: It is important when performing training such as this that the athlete be fully aware of the most efficient movements for the safest execution. As we have stated before ["Correct Technique: Does it Matter?" *MILO*, September 2009, Vol. 17, No. 2] technique does matter. Start slowly, experiment carefully, and pay close attention to your form. If technique or sloppy attempts are made with any highly intense exercise, the risk of injury increases drastically. Be safe as you train.

Harness or rope pull

After lashing together the logs, attach the rope to a harness (or simply throw it over your shoulder), grip hard, and pull. A harness will allow for a more forward lean and use of your hands on the ground for assistance. Without the harness you are forced to use your grip on the rope and you must also use your torso in a different manner, as it is twisted and tugged by the logs as they grind against the ground.

Harness pull.
Photos courtesy of Tim Piper.

Rope pull.

Back drag

To perform a back drag, place one end of the log on one shoulder and drag the other end of the log on the ground.

This is a variation of the forward pull already described, but it requires much more arm strength as the hands have to keep the log in place throughout the exercise.

Backward pull.

Backward pull and sideways pull

The backward pull is a great way to isolate the legs and posterior chain. As you lean against the rope and draw out the slack, you begin to feel the work in the spinal erectors. As you start your backward march, your legs will really feel the burn. The sideways pull stresses the inner and outer thighs while simultaneously working the torso as you twist and turn with each step.

Yoke walk

Most are familiar with this exercise from strongman competitions; in most of these meets the yoke walk begins much like a squat. However, when using logs, you have to first get the log into position on your back yourself.

After experimentation, we have found that the best way to situate the log on the shoulders is to employ a technique borrowed from the USAWA—the Steinborn lift. The basic idea is to tilt the log onto one end, assume a deep squat, brace the closest shoulder against the log, and slowly lower the log to a position across both shoulders; slowly stand up and begin to walk.

Steinborn lift setup.

Yoke walk with log.

Yoke lunge and monster walks

After getting the log into position on the shoulders, perform lunges. A more intense variation is the walking lunge, what many in our region refer to as monster walks. This requires a high degree of control and attention to each and every step as you trudge across what is usually a very uneven field or pasture.

Yoke monster walk and twist.

Yoke monster walk and twist

The yoke monster walk and twist is likely the most intense and dangerous exercise of them all: any attempt with this exercise is done strictly at your own risk. The monster walk part of the movement is performed the same way as described in the exercise above. For the twist, when in the lowest position you slowly rotate the torso until one end of the log points toward the ground. Once you have twisted safely as far as possible, slowly untwist the spine and then proceed with another step forward. Upon completing the next step you twist to the opposite side. When performed carefully, this exercise can be very useful for strongman competitors, wrestlers, MMA athletes, or anyone in sports who requires total body strength in awkward positions. Assuming a lunge position and then rotating your spine while under a load is a risky practice; again, use caution and do this only at your own risk.

Draft horse-style training has been one of the most interesting and fun accidental discoveries we have encountered. While we are always excited to try new exercises, we must caution you that while the pulls seem relatively safe, the yoke exercises are more challenging. If you choose to try them, start slowly and carefully. Build up as time goes on and above all, don't forget that as far as technique goes . . . it *does* matter.

You Are What You Don't Eat:
Organic Food and the Strength Athlete, Part II

Gabriel Josiah

On a hot summer day a while back I was looking inside the gutters around our house. They were filled about an inch thick with charcoal-looking, caked-on crud that had probably been in there for 15 years. I'm a vacuum freak. Totally love it. I think that the shop vac is the greatest invention since the can opener. If it moves, I'll vacuum it. If it doesn't move, I'll vacuum it. Dirty floor? Vacuum it. Spider web in the corner of the ceiling? Vacuum it. Ant problem? Vacuum it. Don't make friends easily? Vacuum it. My neighbors just shake their heads when they see me shop-vaccing the grass debris on the sidewalk after mowing.

So, armed with a 6-hp Craftsman shop vac, an extension ladder, and a set of steady nerves for crawling around on the roof, I started cleaning out the gutters. After filling up the shop vac with gutter gunk, I began to think (something that has become a habit—keeps the brain strong) how many people's insides look like the inside of those gutters. How many people have toxic waste material built up in their bodies because of toxins contained in the food they've eaten for the last 10 or 15 years, or even a lifetime? Last June, we looked at the benefits of an organic diet ("Organic Food and the Strength Athlete," MILO, Vol. 17, No. 1). I hope to build on that foundation and to address some misconceptions people have about eating an organic diet.

It is my contention that not only "you are what you eat," but also, "you are what you *don't* eat." Good health is just as much keeping the bad things out as it is putting the good things in. Before we go any further, let's define "good health." In *Keys to Progress* John McCallum wrote, tongue-in-cheek, "To the average guy on the street, good health means four colds a year and the flu every winter. It means a major illness once in five years and a major operation in ten. It means pills so his head won't ache . . . pills to make him sleep and pills to keep him awake. It means giving up his teeth at thirty, his hair at forty, and the ghost at fifty. It means, in short, a condition more to be endured than enjoyed. Good health to the average man isn't really all that good."

John states that this is *not* good health, and I agree with him. Good health means an absence of all aches, pains, headaches, and diseases (including colds and flu). It means sound sleep at night, plentiful energy during the day, speedy recovery from cuts, bruises, and muscle strains, never seeing the inside of a hospital except to visit sick friends, and being free from taking any prescription and non-prescrip-

> GOOD HEALTH IS SOMETHING GOD CREATED THE HUMAN BODY TO ENJOY.

tion drugs. Good health is something God created the human body to enjoy.

I believe good health is built on two things: (a) what you put in your body, and (b) what you keep out. Let's look at both of these in the context of eating organic food.

What you put in: "You are what you eat."

"All food is medicine, and the best food is the best medicine."—Hippocrates, father of medicine

Have you ever noticed how almost every month there seems to be some new food-based supplement introduced to the public? Garlic pills, noni juice, pomegranate juice, psyllium seed husk fiber, acai juice, cod liver oil, grape seed extract, spirulina, wheat grass powder, green tea, nopal superfruit concentrate. Each one claims an abundance of health benefits to its consumers. Ever wonder which one is right? I'm going to shock you. To a certain extent, *they all are.* That's because wholesome, nutritious foods (and food-based supplements) have the ability to heal. Let me clarify. I'm not saying that all these supplements are magic pills, but they all, to a certain extent, assist the body in achieving and maintaining good health. It goes without saying that if you constantly shovel junk (bleached white bread, deep fried foods, cookies, candy, ice cream, donuts, sugar, sugar, sugar) into your gut, you won't acquire, much less maintain, good health. So the first step is to eat wholesome, nutritious foods. You know the kind: a generous supply of fruits, vegetables, nuts, cheeses, eggs, and healthy meats. But, I'm making a case for organic food, so let's look at the benefits of eating these wholesome foods in their organic form.

There are numerous studies showing the superiority of organic food over conventional food in terms of nutritional content. As a rule, organic food has many times the nutritional value that conventional food has. For example, organic milk has significantly higher levels of conjugated linoleic acid (CLA) than conventional milk. Potential benefits of CLA are: reducing the body's propensity to store fat, inhibiting tumor development, and increasing immune response against viral antigens. Organic milk also has up to 70% more omega 3s (good fats) than conventional milk, is two to three times richer in the antioxidants lutein and zeaxanthin (important for eye health), and has on average 50% more vitamin E and 75% more beta carotene (which the body converts to vitamin A).[1]

The organic advantage doesn't stop at dairy. Organic spinach (good for forearms like Popeye) contains higher levels of flavonoids and vitamin C with lower levels of nitrates (which can be a catalyst to cancer). Organic tomatoes are higher in flavonoids, lycopene, and vitamin C. A four-year EU study found that all organic produce has up to 40% more antioxidants than their conventional counterparts.

Why the dramatic nutritional difference? Organic farmers recognize that food is only as good as the soil in which it is grown. Therefore they choose to nurture the soil by not using synthetic chemical fertilizers, pesticides and herbicides, and by recognizing the need for algae, bacteria, fungi, protozoa, and other life forms, like earthworms, to be present. In addition, organic farming relies heavily on crop cover and mulching, which tend to preserve valuable topsoil. All

> ORGANIC FARMERS RECOGNIZE THAT FOOD IS ONLY AS GOOD AS THE SOIL IN WHICH IT IS GROWN.

of this results in crops that use soil nutrients more effectively. George Vojkovich, a certified organic rancher from Washington State says, "Our bodies are a soil by-product. Over the last 50 years, factory farming achieved mass production of cheap food, but devastated the sustainability of farmland. We have beautiful vegetables that are void of nutrients, (and) meats that have been pumped up with hormones and antibiotics." To combat this problem (and his own irregular heartbeat), George Vojkovich became a certified organic rancher.

Paula Baillie-Hamilton, M.D., Ph.D. says that for thousands of years "our bodies used the relative abundance of nutrients and the naturally high fiber content of our diet to neutralize existing chemical threats. Today we still need the same high level of nutrients—vitamins, minerals, and essential fatty acids—and fiber to detoxify and remove toxins. However, our modern, highly refined diets contain only a fraction of the nutrients and fiber they once did." She states that the dramatic increase in the amount of heavy metals and synthetic chemicals in our foods results in our bodies being "exposed to levels of chemicals far higher than our bodies were designed to withstand."[2] Eating 100% organic food ensures that you are getting the most bang for your nutritional buck. It ensures that the food you are putting in your body has the highest nutritional content available and therefore the greatest health potential.

God said, "See, I have given you every herb that yields seed which is on the face of all the earth, and every tree whose fruit yields seed; to you it shall be for food."—Genesis 1:29

What you keep out: "You are what you don't eat."

Food plays a pivotal role in the strength athlete's regimen. It takes good food, and lots of it, to build strength and size. Weightlifters are the only people on earth who eat between bites. Because strength athletes, as a rule, consume copious quantities of grub, the quality of food they consume must be considered. The case for pure, chemical-free food is not a new one. In 1902 Harvey Wiley, chief chemist of the U.S. Department of Agriculture, began a series of tests on volunteers to see whether the allegations against some of the era's most commonly-used preservatives were true. He added minute traces (tiny amounts) of such substances as borax, benzoic acid, and formaldehyde to the otherwise untainted food eaten by his subjects. The chemicals, Wiley discovered, did indeed produce adverse health effects. Some of the men lost their appetite and became nauseated and had to be taken off the doctored diets. Wiley soon began heading a movement to reform the food industry.[3]

Organic food keeps out chemicals, pesticides, and preservatives—toxins. You might say, "Well, big deal. What's wrong with a few toxins in my food?" The toxins contained in our food, especially pesticides, take up residence in our fatty tissues. Our brains contain a form of fat called phospholipids. Our nerve cells are encased in a membrane consisting of phospholipids. Many toxins are fat-soluble and thus can *accumulate* in fatty tissues and in cell membranes, including our brains.[4] I highlight accumulate for a good reason. Unless you (a) are on a continuous, rigorous detoxification program to rid yourself of these toxins, or (b) have achieved a remarkable body fat percentage of zero, they can and will accumulate in your body and cause health problems.

Disease occurs when the body can no longer keep up with the toxins it is being exposed to on a daily basis. In 2002, a peer-reviewed scientific journal published a comparison of pesticide residues in organic and non-organic foods. From the 94,000 food samples they analyzed, they found that organic foods contain far fewer pesticide residues than conventional foods.[5] Eating organic is a simple and effective way to drastically reduce your body's toxic load. It keeps the junk out, thus giving your body its best chance to spend its time building and maintaining health, rather than always having to fight sickness.

Misconceptions

In closing, let's address a few specific misconceptions I have heard about eating organic.

"It doesn't matter what foods I eat, as long as they are organic."

False. An organic cookie is still a cookie, a high-sugar treat to be eaten in moderation. It is, however, much more beneficial and healthful than the Oreo. Fruits, vegetables, nuts, seeds, and the like are always the best health choice.

"The 'USDA organic' label means nothing."

False. Let's just look at organic meat. George Vojkovich, the organic rancher whom I mentioned earlier, became certified organic in 2000. What does this certification entail? Let me tell you, it's a whole lot more than just slapping a "USDA organic" sticker on his food. What this certification means to him is a prohibition of all chemicals (herbicides, insecticides, fungicides, synthetic fertilizers, treated seeds) on or near his fields for at least three years before he can be certified; a prohibition of the use of antibiotics, synthetic hormones, and most conventional pharmaceuticals; adequate record-keeping to verify land management practices; access to pasture for all cattle; and moving the cattle from pasture to pasture, which allows the grass to recover.

"Organic produce is subject to the same 'depleted soil' that conventional produce is subject to."

False. Depleted soil occurs from years of mass overproduction of crops and the use of pesticides. Organic farming avoids this problem by (a) using crop rotation, which allows the land to rest and recover, (b) not using mineral-depleting pesticides and chemicals, and (c) and 'nurturing' the land with careful farming practices. The very fact that organic produce has many times more nutritional value than conventional produce should speak volumes about the quality of soil in which it's being grown.

> AN ORGANIC COOKIE IS STILL A COOKIE, A HIGH-SUGAR TREAT TO BE EATEN IN MODERATION.

Dr. Don Colbert, M.D. says, "We live and die because of the food we place in our bodies. It is imperative that we become more disciplined and make the right dietary choices." So, begin making the right dietary choices by eating healthy, pure, organic food. And by the way, this is one situation where a shop vac won't help. ∎

Notes:
1. "Organic Milk 'Higher in Vitamins,'" BBC News, 1/7/05.
2. *Taste for Life*, (Connell Communications, Inc., April 2006), p. 18.
3. *Wholesome Diet* (Time-Life Books, 1981), pp. 123–125.
4. Don Colbert, M.D., *What You Don't Know May Be Killing You* (Siloam Press, 2000), p. 45.
5. B. P. Baker et al., "Pesticide Residues in Conventional, Integrated Pest Management (IPM)-grown and Organic Foods: Insight from Three U.S. Data Sets," *Food Additives and Contaminants* 19 (2002): pp. 427–446

Basketball Rebounding for Coordination, Quickness, and Agility

Col. (Ret.) Joseph H. Wolfenberger

For lack of a better name, I'll call the exercise I'm about to describe and highly recommend basketball rebounding. I have a vivid memory of many years ago when I happened to see and buy the magazine *Muscle Power*, edited by Earle E. Liederman. Liederman had been an outstanding wrestler and athlete and always recommended well-rounded physical development. Being fairly athletic and competitive, I resolved early on to use my muscles in a balanced way (other than just for lifting and bodybuilding). Weight training during that period was a big factor in my becoming co-captain of the high school football team and fairly proficient in track and field events (shot put and discus) and in golf (at an early age my dad took me to the local golf course to earn some money caddying). Later I played football in college and in the army.

By that time I had developed a strong belief that the basic lifting motions (cleans, snatches, jerks, squats, rowing, etc.) were the best exercises to develop all-around athletic ability. After a while, during a long military career in the army (I retired with over 30 years service as a colonel), I got into martial arts (karate) and discovered there were other exercises that developed quickness, power, and explosiveness. The basketball rebounding exercise is one of those movements that I feel is particularly valuable, especially if you normally train alone as I do.

To perform this exercise, you need a basketball and a strong wall to bounce the ball against. In my own case, I screwed a 4' x 6' piece of 3/4" plywood to one of my garage walls where I work out. This is important because you'll see by the explanation that this is not a namby-pamby exercise. You have to put considerable effort into it to reap its benefits.

Rebound board set-up.
Photos courtesy of Joseph H. Wolfenberger.

Begin by standing 6 to 10 feet from your rebound board with both hands on the ball, with your arms against your chest, feet comfortably apart, and knees bent. Vigorously extend your bent arms and wrists and your legs, causing the ball to travel forward rapidly and forcefully and bounce off the wall. Retrieve the ball and repeat. Perform 6 to 12 reps, trying to increase the force of the motion as you build reps.

For the second variation, hold the ball in one hand or the other, with your arm cocked and your body at an angle (as if you were going to throw a baseball). Throw the ball hard against the rebound board; retrieve and repeat 6 to

Starting position for the two-arm throw.

One-arm throw.

12 times. Perform the same motion and reps with the other arm.

Lastly, hold the ball in one hand, low against the body, with the body canted (as if you were going to throw a softball underhand). Throw the ball underhand hard against the wall board, retrieve and repeat for 6 to 12 reps or more. For this variation, try to throw the ball at different angles against the rebound board, causing the ball to return in different paths. This will force you to move your feet a lot, enhancing agility.

Underhand throw.

In all of these motions, try to keep the ball moving almost constantly as this will definitely increase the overall benefits of the exercise.

If you are any kind of an athlete, I believe you will be surprised at the benefits that basketball rebounding will produce. It is inevitable that as we get older, our reflexes get slower. The basketball rebounding exercise will help to counter this trend. In my own case, I still retain considerable punching and kicking power and am still considered a fairly long driver of the golf ball. I attribute these skills to performing exercises such as this one, as well as an all-around weight training program.

Roadrash:
Playing Around with the Push Sled—Part II

Matt Shatzkin Lieutenant Colonel, U.S. Army
Commander, 407th Brigade Support Battalion
2nd Brigade Combat Team, 82nd Airborne Division

In the army we have a saying: "Always improve your position." While this refers to the process of constantly refining defensive positions, we also apply this mindset toward continuous process improvement for maximum combat readiness—which starts with physical readiness.

While we love [the workout] "Albritton" (see "Playing Around with the Push Sled," MILO March 2009, Vol. 16, No. 4), we knew we couldn't stop there. "Albritton," requiring a seven-man push sled located almost two miles away from our headquarters, necessitated too much planning and time. Knowing that lack of proximity and access were obstacles to execution, we knew we had to do better.

We commissioned a high-speed welder within our organization to build our own smaller but equally lethal sleds so we could have these beasts parked right at our headquarters, ready to be pushed in an instant. Wanting to break them in right, we asked for them to be ready by a certain date, and then arranged for our brigade leadership team, along with our all company leadership teams, to come give them a whirl.

Unfortunately, when developing new recipes, you're going to break some eggs. While breaking into this new territory, things didn't go as smoothly as planned. We found that the skis of the sled were too thin, causing the sled to get stuck after only 2 to 3 feet of pushing. While we knew we needed wider skis, we also knew we were running out of time. So we set out to devise an alternate plan . . . at 8:30 p.m. the night prior to our scheduled workout.

Our battalion command sergeant-major, two captains and I went out to "the yard" (our new term for our workout area, just outside our headquarters) for inspiration. We resembled several jazz musicians getting together to improvise. Armed with our CrossFit knowledge and experience developing team workouts, we went to work. We picked up two 60-lb. pails and yoked them through a crossbeam. Nope, wouldn't last. We ran a crossbeam through four tires. OK, now what? We ran a strap through a tire and dragged it. Too light. Two tires. Getting somewhere. Three tires—now we were on to something. After about thirty minutes, we had a plan we felt pretty good about.

> WE RESEMBLED SEVERAL JAZZ MUSICIANS GETTING TOGETHER TO IMPROVISE.

Heat 1 kicks off with plenty of intensity.

First Sergeant Jones delivers the goods.

Lt. Col. Matt Shatzkin prepares to take over the heavy bag.

Team 3 cranks through the knees-to-elbows drill.

The Falcon Brigade Combat Team Commander, Col. Christopher Gibson, puts the bottle through for a bonus-round credit.

Here's what we devised:

Teams of three to perform as many rounds as possible in 30 minutes

- "Conga line" 3-tire drag for 50 meters
- simultaneous performance of 15 knees-to-elbows (team total must equal 15, with each member performing one repetition)
- simultaneous performance of 15 lunges (team total must equal 15, with each member performing one repetition; 10 of 15 reps must be weighted with a 50-lb. duffel bag on the shoulder; team has one bag to work with)
- the great "equalizer" (our favorite)—at the end of each round, the team gets one chance to throw a plastic bottle through a vertical tire; a throw through the tire earns a two-round credit for the price of one, and a miss only counts for one round

The next morning brought some rain, some mud, some blood, and a whole lot of fun. We livened up things with the help of Francine, our portable audio system that packs an absolute wallop, particularly when we arm her with the likes of Terror, Rollins Band and other hardcore music selections to really ramp up the intensity. Of our four teams, two of them tied with 14 rounds apiece, with all teams thoroughly enjoying the competition. Due to the tires, skinned shins and blistered hands from pulling cargo straps, our teams happily dubbed their new favorite workout "Roadrash."

One person's crisis is another's opportunity. The dilemma of not having our sleds ready forced us to get back to the innovations of the drawing board and as a result, we were rewarded with two stellar workouts for the price of one. Our welders are still driving on with perfecting the three-man sled—we anticipate unleashing "the Dark Dog" within the next 30 days!

> ONE PERSON'S CRISIS IS ANOTHER'S OPPORTUNITY.

The Push–Pull of Things

John Brookfield

Author of *Mastery of Hand Strength, Revised Edition,*
The Grip Master's Manual, Training with Cables for
Strength, and *Dexterity Ball Training for Hands*

In this article I will show you an approach to strength training that you have never seen before. The method is extremely deceptive not only in its difficulty, but also in the results it will produce from steady training. Many of you are familiar with my battling ropes training system: it is vast and has many different concepts and applications. The push–pull strength concept is what we will examine today.

The push–pull concept of the Battling Ropes system is very similar to the basic exercises done with barbells and dumbbells; however, the feel of the movements will be quite different. Every traditional exercise with iron can be simulated with ropes in the push–pull method. The big difference is that you will be, as the title indicates, pushing and pulling at the same time—which I am sure sounds impossible to most of you. The concept of pushing and pulling at the same time has not been done before and can only be simulated in the battling ropes

> THE BIG DIFFERENCE IS THAT YOU WILL BE, AS THE TITLE INDICATES, PUSHING AND PULLING AT THE SAME TIME—WHICH I AM SURE SOUNDS IMPOSSIBLE TO MOST OF YOU.

program. The method is completely safe and easy to set up, and it can be used by anyone at any level.

As far as setup and equipment, I suggest using a 50-ft. rope—either manila or poly—that is 1-1/2" in diameter. A 50-ft. 1-1/2" piece of manila rope will weigh about 50 lb. and a 50-ft. 1-1/2" piece of poly rope will weigh about 22 lb. A heavier rope, such as a 50-ft. 2"-diameter rope, can also be used; however, the standard 1-1/2" rope will be plenty.

You will also need an anchor point, such as a pole in the ground, a goal post or a sturdy rack of some kind—even a tree will work; however, make sure that your anchor point is not so sharp that it cuts into your rope. Once you have established your anchor point, take the 50-ft. rope and bring it around the anchor point so that you have two equal lengths extending from each side. Bring the ends of the rope together, stretching out the rope completely and taking up the slack, keeping the ends equal in length. Also, make sure that your anchor point and rope are on the ground or at least within a few inches of the ground—don't have the rope elevated too high off the ground for the training.

Now you are ready to go to work. Even though there are many exercises that can be done with the push–pull system (the crucifix is also a good one), let's start with the standard military press or overhead press. To start, grab the rope with one end in one hand and the other end in the other hand. You will have to play a bit with the tension to find the best level to start; however, I would suggest grabbing the rope toward the ends to get a feel for the movement. Grasping the rope tightly, step back so that you take up the slack in the rope. From here, pull back with your arms so that the entire rope is off the ground; if any of the rope is resting on the ground you need to pull back harder with your upper body so that the entire rope is elevated slightly.

Here's where you start both pulling and pushing: with the rope off the ground, simultaneously pull back on the rope while pressing or pushing it overhead. You will notice that the rope will go slightly in front of you instead of completely overhead. You will also notice that this method is very difficult and demanding for anyone at any level—your body and mind have to stay completely engaged at all times in order to keep the rope off the ground throughout the exercise. Once you press the rope overhead, slowly lower it back to the starting point and then press it up again. Continue pressing and lowering the rope the same way that you would a pair of dumbbells or a barbell. Remember, you must keep the rope off the ground throughout the entire movement, and the only way this is possible is to keep pulling back and keep constant tension on the rope at all times.

This push–pull method works your muscles in a totally unique and effective way—a way that you likely have never experienced before. You will really have to fight the fatigue from the constant stress put on the muscles. When doing the standard military or overhead press, you may need to make

Pulling the ropes to keep them off the ground.
Photos courtesy of John Brookfield.

Pushing the ropes overhead.

adjustments with your body to get the right positioning.

Because of the length of the rope, you can do a heavy or light workout. Consider your rope like a rack of dumbbells or a barbell to which you can add or subtract weight. To vary the difficulty of the exercise, you can change the tension of the rope by changing your position relative to the anchor point: if you move closer to the anchor point the tension is lighter, if you move farther toward the ends of the rope, the movement is harder and rope is heavier. This is where the rack of dumbbells comes into play, so to speak: you can do sets the same way you would with weights. You can do a warm-up set by moving close to the anchor point, and then go heavier and heavier as you move farther from the anchor point.

Often I do ladders or pyramids by going up and down the rope. For example, I do a set of 5 reps at the ends of the rope; move a foot closer to the anchor point of the rope and do 5 more reps; move another foot closer and do 5 more reps, continuing all the way to the anchor point. From there I back up, increasing the workload again as I get farther away from the anchor point.

You can decide how much tension you wish to apply and how many sets or reps you wish to do each time. The main thing to remember is to pull back and see that the ropes are off the ground before pushing overhead. Without the visual reminder of seeing that the ropes are off the ground, your mind won't understand the concept of pushing and pulling at the same time. If you can't keep the ropes off the ground throughout the movement, you are trying to handle too much tension, and you should move closer to the anchor point. Once you get stronger, try moving backward again, away from the anchor point, in order to increase the tension. This, of course, is like adding weight to a dumbbell or barbell.

> OFTEN I DO LADDERS OR PYRAMIDS BY GOING UP AND DOWN THE ROPE.

Don't be discouraged if you can't handle the full length of the rope in the beginning. Just concentrate on the pulling back and pushing overhead concept at first. You will soon get stronger and be able to handle more tension on the rope.

Good luck with the push-pull. **M**

Pushing (Back at) 40

Steve Brylski

It's been a few years since I've written for *MILO*. I've been pretty busy with my career while I've been out of the fold. However, I still enjoy training, and I'd like to share with the readers of *MILO* what I'm currently doing in the gym.

Several months back, I turned 39. Granted, this is not one of those birthdays with a "zero" in it that makes you re-examine every aspect of your life up to that point, but it was close for me at least. I decided that I needed to make a careful study of where I was physically, where I wanted to go with my training, and how I needed to live my life going forward. Luckily for me, having trained with weights for 23 years and being fairly well-read on the topic of strength training, I had a healthy body of knowledge to draw from. After many years of trial and error, I know what works best for me, what exercises I enjoy the most, and what types of things I know I must do (even if they're not my favorite things to do). I wanted to create a workout that was challenging and which would allow me to gain size and strength. I sat down with a pad and pencil and mapped out a workout that, after some tweaks here and there, I'm still doing to this day.

> Hey, just because you're closing in on the big four-O, doesn't mean you can't train to gain.

What follows is the current workout from which I've been getting some really solid results. It's a three-day-a-week program that emphasizes some mass-building exercises and general physical preparedness work. Hey, just because you're closing in on the big four-O, doesn't mean you can't train to gain. Save the rocking-chair mentality for when you hit 80 plus. That being said, let's get to it.

Day one – chins, standing presses, one-arm dumbbell rows, farmer's walk, complex training

Day one begins on one of the most valuable pieces of equipment in any gym: the chin-up bar. If you remember any of my articles from years past, you'll know that I'm a huge proponent of this movement. Flat out, it can really pack on the muscle in a relatively short amount of time. I like to begin the workout with a predetermined number of supinated grip chin-ups, usually between 25 to 40 total reps, which I try to accomplish in the fewest number of sets as possible. I try to take no more than 45 seconds of rest between sets. You really want to push yourself on these—try to grind out as many reps as you can. As you get better conditioned, you'll be able to do the reps in fewer and fewer sets.

After completing the predetermined number of reps, I like to do a three-part static contraction set, which works three different parts of the chin-up movement: the top, three-quarters up, and halfway up. This can be very tough, especially when you're in a pre-fatigued state. I like to do holds of 10 seconds, but you might want to start off with 5 seconds in order to get used to these. One "set" would be performed as follows: complete a full-range chin-up and then hold yourself at the top of the movement (trying to get your chest pressed up to the bar) for a 10 count. When you're done, lower yourself to the floor, take 3 deep breaths, and then chin yourself to the three-quarters point of the movement (near completion) and hold yourself there for another 10 count. After lowering yourself to the floor once again, take 3 more deep breaths; then chin yourself to the halfway point of the movement and count off another 10 seconds. This protocol is deceptively tough, and should work you over pretty well. Try to do 4 sets of these. As noted earlier, if 10 seconds is too much for you to start with, try 5 seconds. You'll still get a lot of benefit from the work.

Next, I like to work the standing press. In the pantheon of exercises, this movement has always held a special place in my heart. This is the exercise that strong men of old cut their teeth on. I've always found that for me, at least, lower reps translated into bigger gains, so I generally won't do any sets that go more than 5 reps with these. The rep scheme that I've been doing lately is 5 sets of 3 reps. I've been getting some nice results based on the protocol outlined below.

To begin with, you'll need to accurately determine your 1-rep max in this movement. When I say 1-rep max, I mean the weight that you can do without cheating, i.e., excessive back bending, or kicking your legs to gain momentum for the bar. Once you figure out your 1-rep max, you will embark upon a 3-week mini-cycle: week 1 you'll be performing 5 sets of 3 reps at 75% of your 1-rep max; week 2 will be 5 sets of 3 reps at 80% of your 1-rep max; and week 3 will be 5 sets of 3 reps at 85% of your 1-rep max. Week 3 should be really hard to complete. You'll probably feel pretty worked over by the end of it. During week 4, you retest your 1-rep max to see where you stand (at which point you will have to recalculate your weights for the next 3 weeks).

Let's say that your 1-rep max is 200 lb. Week 1 (75%) would be 5 sets of 3 reps at 150 lb. Week 2 (80%) would be 5 sets of 3 reps at 160 lb. Week 3 (85%) would be 5 sets of 3 reps at 170 lb. Always use good form in order to get the most out of this movement.

After presses, I like to do a couple of tough sets of one-arm dumbbell rows. Generally, I do one of two different rep schemes for this exercise. Sometimes I prefer to do 1 set of 10 reps followed by another heavier set of 6 reps. Other times, when I want to use slightly heavier weights, I will do 1 set of 8 reps followed by a second heavier set of 5 reps. Either scheme should put you on the path to muscle growth. Try them both and see which one works best for you.

To finish off the weights portion of day one, I like to do a couple of sets of farmer's walks. If you're not familiar with this exercise, it's quite simple to learn: you take a heavy dumbbell in each hand and walk until your grip is fried and you have to put down the weight and rest. The feeling that washes over you at that point is called (temporary) relief. Your arms will feel light, almost as if your hands were attached to two balloons. After you catch your breath, pick up the dumbbells again and take them for another stroll. You should feel pretty worked over by this point. I've always considered this exercise a "man-maker" (no offense to the ladies of MILO . . . I love ya).

I like to conclude my day one training with some energy system work.

Now that I'm pushing 40, I've increased the amount of so-called "energy system training" that I do. I know that I need to be more heart-friendly in my approach to exercise. My family has a history of heart disease so this is a necessity (and a no-brainer) for me.

Back when I dabbled in the Olympic lifts, I became quite fascinated with complex training movements. You'll definitely see the influence they had on my training if you read some of my old MILO articles. Complex training really helped me slim down and to get into better shape. Anyway, I wanted to adapt the complex-type training model to my energy system training. I wanted to do something that was fun, yet challenging enough to make me sweat and get my heart rate going.

I came up with the following, which I do after my day one and day three workouts. The only piece of equipment that you'll need is a good old-fashioned jump rope. Jumping rope isn't just for kids anymore! That being said, I like to do 8 "periods" of work in a complex training manner. The first part of the complex is to do a set of jumping rope to failure, i.e., do as many skips as you can before you fail (the rope hits your feet). Then, immediately follow this with a set of squat thrusts, squat jumps, slalom jumps, or jumping jacks, for a predetermined number of reps. This would equal one "period."

> THE FEELING THAT WASHES OVER YOU AT THAT POINT IS CALLED (TEMPORARY) RELIEF.

This is how I do it. I perform 8 periods in the following manner (which you can change based on your preferences):

Periods 1 – 4

- jump rope to failure + 5 squat thrusts (remember these from gym class?—also called burpees)
- jump rope to failure + 5 squat jumps (bend your knees and do a vertical jump)
- jump rope to failure + 25 jumping jacks
- jump rope to failure + 10 slalom jumps (pick a point on the ground and jump over it laterally with your feet together; do this back and forth over the line until you reach the prescribed reps)

Periods 5 through 8 are simply repeats of periods 1 through 4.

I've had some fun with this. Sometimes I'll do some different exercises, like mountain climbers, medicine ball slams, or stair runs. As you become more proficient with the rope, these complexes will become harder—but by and large, I think that you'll learn to enjoy them.

Day two – 5 x 5 strength-building model: 30-degree incline presses, seated rows, squats, treadmill

Day two of the workout is fairly simple. It's a total nod to the classic 5 x 5 strength-building model. I only perform three exercises, but I work them hard. To begin the workout, I like to do 30-degree incline presses. This exercise has always treated me well. I perform the 5 sets as follows: set 1 is a warm-up; set 2 is a heavier warm-up set; and sets 3 through 5 are the work sets. I generally use the same weight for the 3 work sets. The idea here is to find a weight that will really challenge you and make the last rep of the 5 sets a near gut-busting effort.

After doing the incline presses, I like to do a seated row movement. If you're big on bent-over barbell rows, they could easily be substituted in place of seated rows. Either way, do the 5 sets of 5 in the same manner as the incline presses.

The last exercise of the day is the squat. Back squat or front squat, they're both equally effective for bringing the pain. We all know that if you don't do squats, you are a bad person who is generally unlikable as a human being. What you didn't know is that the following events might also occur: a) the IRS will audit your last 10 tax returns; b) your dog will leave a little "surprise" in your favorite pair of shoes; and c) your mother-in-law might accidentally drive off a cliff . . . in your brand new car (on which you still owe many payments).

> THE IDEA HERE IS TO FIND A WEIGHT THAT WILL REALLY CHALLENGE YOU AND MAKE THE LAST REP OF THE 5 SETS A NEAR GUT-BUSTING EFFORT.

Okay, so maybe none of the above is actually true—besides the bringing the pain part. Five sets of 5 in the squat is a tough deal, but stick with it and you'll be rewarded with some great results.

I end my day two workout with some treadmill work. After a sufficient warm-up of about 15 minutes at a moderate speed on the treadmill, I like to incrementally increase the speed until I end up in a good sprint. Basically, I will increase the rate of speed on the treadmill by 3/10 mph every minute until I get to a full sprint, which I'll do for as long as I can stand it. If your warm-up was done at 4.0 mph, you would go up to 4.3 mph, 4.6, 4.9, 5.2, and so on, until you were running in full stride. When you end your sprint, lower the speed back down to what you warmed up with and do a 10-minute cool-down. Always exercise caution on the treadmill (of course).

Day three – weighted chin-ups, weighted chest dips, complex training

Day three is all about two exercises: the weighted supinated lat chin-up and the weighted chest dip. The goal is to get to a point where you're handling some respectable weights on both of these exercises. You already know about the chin-up. The weighted chest dip is affectionately known as the "upper body squat" for its propensity to pack on mass to your chest, shoulders, and arms. For this workout you will need a quality dip belt, something that will stand up to the rigors of time and heavy effort.

I begin day three by working the chin-up. I believe that weighted chins could cause some elbow problems if you try to do too many reps per set; for that reason, I keep my sets to a maximum of 3 reps. Currently weighing in at 240 lb., I approach my workout in the following manner. I start out easy (I'm talking about a 10-lb. plate) and do 3 reps. It's nice to start off with an easy warm-up—it primes the pump, in a manner of speaking. I then continue to go up 10 lb. every set. Once I can't get 3 reps on a set, I dial it back to 2 reps. Finally, when I can't get 2 reps with a weight, I go for singles until I can't even do a single rep.

If you were doing this workout, it might look something like this for you:

+ 10 x 3; + 20 x 3; + 30 x 3; + 40 x 3; + 50 x 2; + 60 x 1; + 70 x 1.

Since I generally do this particular workout on Saturdays, I take slightly more generous rest periods between sets, but I certainly don't loaf through the workout. I enjoy this day the most since I can get to the gym early (7:30-ish) when it's not crowded, and get in some quality strength work.

If you can't do weighted chin-ups, you should work the lat pulldown machine with a purpose, doing the same rep schemes described above. Once you get strong enough, you'll be able to switch over to the weighted chin-up.

I do like to throw in a finisher set or two of half chin-ups after I'm done with weighted chins. These are performed as follows: the first rep is a full chin-up; lower down half way, and immediately pull yourself back up to the top. Repeatedly lower halfway down and then pull yourself back up to the top for the predetermined number of reps. I like to do a couple of sets of 5 reps with these. I find that this movement really helps with the top portion of the chin-up, if that's your sticking point.

Moving on to weighted dips is next. I do a couple of sets with bodyweight just to get my dipping muscles prepped for the upcoming work. With weighted dips, I've always felt that sets of 5 were the perfect rep scheme to achieve strength and growth, so that's what I stick with. Just as I do with the weighted chins, I start out with 10 lb. and do a set of 5. I then increase the weight by 10 lb. each set. When I can't get 5 reps, I drop my sets down to 3 reps. When I can't get 3 reps, I go down to 2. I finish with heavy singles to failure. If you have a problem doing weighted dips, you should consider substituting close-grip bench presses for them.

I round out day three with my jump rope complexes.

I generally divide my workouts on a Tuesday–Thursday–Saturday schedule. Based on my particular needs, this works best for me. You may need to do things on a different schedule, which is fine. We all have different demands, pressures, and timetables to contend with, so you have to find out what works best for you. I would just caution you to have at least a two-day break between the two chin-up workouts. I think that is the best approach for aiding recovery.

Sunday – active rest: bicycling or walking

I try to make Sundays an active rest day. Recently I've made two important purchases: a really great, comfortable bicycle and a pedometer. Some Sundays I take long bike rides, either along the boardwalk at Long Beach (a town in Long Island, New York which borders the Atlantic Ocean), or along the Hudson River bike path in Manhattan. Bike riding is great exercise and is pretty fun when you get right down to it—it kind of makes you feel like a kid again.

Other Sundays I take some really long walks—like 7 or 8 miles. I get up early, usually 7 a.m. (which is technically "sleeping in" for a person like me who gets up for work at 5 a.m. each day), put on some comfortable walking shoes, grab my portable music player, and walk, and walk, and walk. The pedometer I purchased was a wise $20 investment. It lets me know how many steps I've taken and how far I've actually walked (in miles). I'm now in the habit of clipping it onto my belt each and every day so I know how much I walk on a daily basis. Just knowing that it's there spurs me on to be more active—to take stairs instead of an elevator, to walk to an extra subway station rather than the closest one, for example.

There you have it—a pretty simple 3-day workout for the lifter approaching middle age who still wants to train to gain and get more fit to boot. Good luck! M

> JUST KNOWING THAT IT'S THERE SPURS ME ON TO BE MORE ACTIVE—TO TAKE STAIRS INSTEAD OF AN ELEVATOR, TO WALK TO AN EXTRA SUBWAY STATION RATHER THAN THE CLOSEST ONE, FOR EXAMPLE.

CALENDAR

Check out the Latest News at **www.ironmind.com**, the Strength World's News Source.

2010 United States Armwrestling Association, Inc.

Apr 10	2nd Annual Ronnie Coleman Classic AW, Mesquite, TX
Apr 17	2nd Annual Europa Show of Champions Pro-Am AW Championships, Orlando, Florida
Jul 10	Oklahoma State Pro-Am AW Championships, Anadarko, OK
Jul 24	1st Annual Europa Battle of Champions AW, Hartford, CT
Aug 5-8	2010 USAF Unified National AW Championships, Billings, MT
Aug 14	17th Annual Europa Super Show Pro-Am AW Challenge, Dallas, TX

For more information, contact the USAA, 246 Custer Avenue, Billings, MT 59101; 406-248-4508 or 406-245-1560; www.usarmwrestling.com.

2010 United States All-Round W/L Assn.

For upcoming events and information, contact Bill Clark, 3906 Grace Ellen Drive, Columbia, MO 652021796. USAWA is a drug-free organization.

2010 Powerlifting

For scheduled events, check *Powerlifting USA* magazine. For subscription information, call 800-448-7693 or 805-482-2378.

2009–2010 USA Weightlifting/IWF

Dec 11-13	American Open, Mobile, AL
Feb 26-28	National Junior Championships, Rochester, MN
Mar 7	Arnold Weightlifting Championships, Columbus, OH
Apr 9-11	National Masters WL Championships, Rego Park, NY
Jun 11-13	National WL Championships, Peoria, IL
Jun TBD	Junior World Championships, Plodiv, Bulgaria
Sep 18-30	World WL Championships, Antalya, Turkey
Oct 3-14	Commonwealth Games, Delhi, India
Nov 12-27	Asian Games, Guangzhou, China

For more information on USA Weightlifting contests, please contact 719-866-4508 or www.usaweightlifting.org. For information about international competitions, please visit www.iwf.net.

2010 Highland Games

For schedules of competitions, please see the following websites:
- www.asgf.org
- www.saaa-net.org
- www.highlandnet.com
- www.nasgaweb.com

105-kg World Record Breakers: The King Has Lost His Crown

Jyrki Rantanen
World's Strongest Man 105-kg 2004 runner-up

Some 25 years ago in Mora, Sweden, the all-time great Jon Pall Sigmarsson roared, "The king has lost his crown!" when he won the World's Strongest Man competition and Geoff Capes lost his crown to the new boy.

Since the 105-kg class started in 2004, there has been one king above all: 3-time winner Janne Hartikainen, who has been unbeaten in the lightweight class since 2001 (the wins include 6 golds from the Finnish Championships, and U.S. readers may remember his performance in Boston in 2002).

The 105-kg World Record Breakers, held in Hamina, Finland, started on 31 July 2009. The 2-day competition included the World Record Breakers and the Finnish Championships. Eight events were held, with 19 competitors (12 Finns and 7 international athletes).

The opener was the medley, with 2 x 100-kg sandbag loading followed by a 25-m farmer's carry (with 120 kg in each hand) and 2 flips with the 350-kg tire. The competition started with familiar sound: Janne Hartikainen was in the lead by almost 6 seconds.

Medley results:

Janne Hartikainen	FIN	32.4 sec.
Maris Rozentals	LAT	38.1
Sergey Konyushok	UKR	38.5

After the medley "warm-up," the competitors hit the log, chasing the world record of 162.5 kg. There were no surprises here except Hartikainen's failure with 140 kg. The event was dominated by Konyushok with a very solid press of 155 kg.

Log for max results:

Sergey Konyushok	UKR	155 kg
Maris Rozentals	LAT	152.5
Marius Lalas	LIT	145

The third event for the day was again a world record-chasing farmer's walk with 120 kg in each hand for 70 m. The former record was over 36 seconds, so for the Finnish crowd, things were looking good when Hartikainen blasted the record with his time of 35.83 seconds. The joy didn't last long, though, because after Hartikainen came Lithuanian newcomer Marius Lalas, stopping the clocks with 35.24, and he even dropped the weights once. If you think that was awesome, guess who was the final competitor on the track? Sergey Konyushok crushed the others' dreams with his time of 30.82 seconds, which, of course, is now the new world record.

Farmer's walk results:		
Sergey Konyushok	UKR	30.82 sec.
Marius Lalas	LIT	35.24
Janne Hartikainen	FIN	35.83

The first day of the competition ended with the arm-over-arm truck pull in a light rain, and most of the competitors managed the pull in 26 to 30 seconds—except the Estonian powerhouse Gert Gorsanov, who took this event with a time of 22.84 seconds.

Arm-over-arm truck pull results:		
Gert Gorsanov	EST	22.84 sec.
Marius Lalas	LIT	23.19
Janne Hartikainen	FIN	25.00

At the end of day one the standings were:

Sergey Konyushok	UKR	71 points
Janne Hartikainen	FIN	66.5
Marius Lalas	LIT	66
Gert Gorsanov	EST	63.5
Maris Rozentals	LAT	56
Rami Koski	FIN	53

For the second day the field was cut to 8 Finns for the Finnish Championships trophy.

The second day started with the car walk world record hunt—370 kg for 25 m. Germany's strong-legged Mirko Rothe got the new world record with his time of 17.49 seconds, followed by the overall leaders, Konyushok and Hartikainen.

Car walk results:		
Mirko Rothe	GER	17.49 sec.
Sergey Konyushok	UKR	18.46
Janne Hartikainen	FIN	18.66

The car walk was followed by the Strongman Champions League (SCL) deadlift machine for reps. The weight—332 kg—was from another planet! Rozentals banged out 6 reps and registered a world record. Lalas showed good power with 4 reps, and Sergey just edged out Hartikainen with 2 reps. The weight was unreal—Hartikainen was the only Finn to pull any reps.

SCL deadlift results:		
Maris Rozentals	LAT	6 reps
Marius Lalas	LIT	4
Sergey Konyushok	UKR	3

When there were just two events to go, it looked as if only an injury could drop Sergey from the top platform—he was already 7 points ahead of Hartikainen, and only the Conan's circle and the Atlas stones were left.

The Conan's circle was a 300-kg apparatus carry, and the favorite for the event was Hartikainen, who during his 105-kg career had only lost this event to Alvidas Bratzius. The favorite took

Marius Lalas.
Janne Hartikainen.
Marius Lalas.
Janne Hartikainen.
Maris Rozentals.
Sergey Konyushok.
Sergey Konyushok.

Photos curtesy of
Jyrki Rantanen.

Sergey Konyushok (l.)
and Maris Rozentals (r).

what was his and spoiled the others' joy of sport by carrying the weight for 2-3/4 laps, while the others managed 2 rounds or less. The event also gave Sergey some cold feelings in his spine, because his lead dropped to 4 points before the stones.

Conan's circle results:		
Janne Hartikainen	FIN	55.70 m
Maris Rozentals	LAT	44.54
Marius Lalas	LIT	43.20

The final event was the Atlas stones, where the world record was set in 2004 by yours truly with the time of 31.06 seconds.

The event included 5 stones (weighing 100, 120, 140, 160, and 180 kg) carried from a distance of 4, 3, 2, 1, and 0 metres to a platform 1.2 m high. In the beginning it seemed that I would walk away keeping my world record because most of the guys had problems with the 140- and 160-kg stones. But again there was the new wave from the Baltic countries, and Marius Lalas came and destroyed the record with his time of 26.31 seconds. Lalas was followed by Hartikainen, who came in a rage and was looking to beat the record—unfortunately he made a mistake with 180-kg stone and equalled the former record with the time of 31.06 seconds. Sergey also lifted up the last stone and grabbed the crown from the king in his overall victory. Hartikainen got some balm for his wounds by getting his sixth Finnish Championships trophy.

The competition was refereed by Ilkka Kinnunen and Jani Kolehmainen. Ilkka was also the announcer and, like the competitors, he did a better job on the second day.

105-kg World Record Breakers 2009 final results:		
Sergey Konyushok	UKR	139 points
Janne Hartikainen	FIN	136
Marius Lalas	LIT	135
Maris Rozentals	LAT	125
Gert Gorsanov	EST	102
Mirko Rothe	GER	90

It was nice to see how things have changed. In the 105-kg class it used to be that the Finns were out of reach and had their own competition at the top. Now the icon Hartikainen was the only Finn in the top six, and the international athletes took the world records, too. The feeling in the competition was exciting, and I must say that it awakened some thoughts in me: "Should I make a comeback or send the 'old horse' to the sausage factory." **M**

THE EVENT ALSO GAVE SERGEY SOME COLD FEELINGS IN HIS SPINE, BECAUSE HIS LEAD DROPPED TO 4 POINTS BEFORE THE STONES.

Helmsman of Russian Heavy Athletics:
Count G. I. Ribeaupierre

Joseph Svub

A pioneer in the field of heavy athletics in Russia, Ivan Lebedev [see "Pioneers of Russian Wrestling and Weightlifting: Ivan Lebedev," *MILO*, September 2007, Vol. 15, No. 2], wrote in his book *Tyazolyaya Atletika*: "If we call Dr. V. F. Krayewski an originator of Russian heavy athletics, thereafter Count Georgiy Ivanovitch Ribeaupierre has been its helmsman. This enthusiastic man spent more than one hundred thousand roubles getting Russian weightlifting sports through bad early times and regaining its footing."[1] Lebedev's book was published more than one hundred years ago, and Count Ribeaupierre died in 1916. Nobody was interested in the man, when and where the patron saint of the Russian Olympic movement died, who his ancestors were, or where he was buried. In 2005, the Russian historian V. Voronin found his grave fallen to pieces at the cemetery in Tsarskoye Selo (now Pushkin), with the engraved words on the epitaph "Count Georgiy Ivanovitch Ribeaupierre, died June 4, 1916."

Let's get familiarized with the Count's life and his doings.

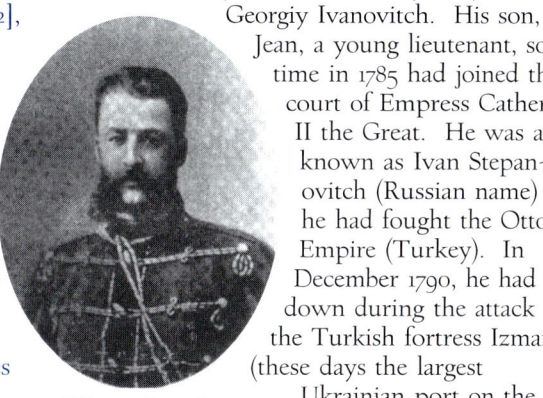

Ribeaupierre in Hussar's uniform

Mark Stefan di Ribeaupierre, a Swiss man and a friend of French philosopher Voltaire, was a great-great-grandfather (in the main family tree) of Georgiy Ivanovitch. His son, Jean, a young lieutenant, sometime in 1785 had joined the court of Empress Catherine II the Great. He was also known as Ivan Stepanovitch (Russian name) and he had fought the Ottoman Empire (Turkey). In December 1790, he had gone down during the attack at the Turkish fortress Izmail (these days the largest Ukrainian port on the Danube Delta).

Alexander, the son of Ivan Stepanovitch, had achieved a high position and financial standing in society either as an administrator of a commercial bank or as an authorized Russian ambassador to Constantinople (now Istanbul) in Turkey. He had considered the import of two Egyptian Sphinxes, around the 1850s, as the most important event in his life. Today they are on display at the Academy of Arts in Saint Petersburg. In 1856, he was elevated to a higher rank, that of count. Alexander's son, Count Ivan Alexandrovitch, had been a high official and a master of ceremony at the court. He had graduated in philosophy and law at the University of Saint Petersburg, later married Soffia Vasilevna Trubecka, and on August 15, 1854, their son Georgiy was born at Tsarskoye Selo. Incidentally, almost two months later, on October 1, a son of the Grand Duchess Catherine II and Grand Duke Peter III, the future Tsar Paul I was born.

Count Ivan spent his boyhood and his adolescent years in Italy and Switzerland. At 12 years old, lessons of gymnastics were given to him by the well-known Italian trainer Rossoti, in Florencia. At 14 years old he trained at Circus Geliom in the most difficult artistic performances, the trapeze exercises, the trampoline, and the double somersault. Later in Switzerland, the young count organized an amateur circus and during the winter he performed at an arena. In the summer, he and his father walked in the Alps, even climbing Mount Blanc. In addition, as a son of noble descent, Georgiy was fully engaged in fencing, shooting, swimming, and horseback riding.

One day, after he reached the age of 15, he saw a performance of professional wrestlers at the marketplace and accepted a challenge to a wrestling match. His first match finished in a tie, and the second one was lost due to his inexperience. Nevertheless, it left a great impression. In 1870, the whole family returned to Russia, and Georgiy enrolled at the illustrious boarding school of Sokolov in Saint Petersburg where he continued his studies. In those days a new sport had become trendy—speed skating, which the count became completely hooked on. Thanks to his fitness level, he quickly appeared to be among the best speed skaters in the city.

In 1873, he was called up to the Kavalergradski Regiment, where he was in charge of preparation of the physical condition of the officers and men, once again thanks to his fitness. When he was transferred to the Life-Guard Horse Regiment of the Empress, a new Russian–Turkish war had begun, so Lieutenant Ribeaupierre voluntarily went to Balkan front-line duty. His superior officers witnessed that he had been fighting with "fearless bravery," which the following story also demonstrates. During one of the attacks, his horse tripped and the wounded count fell down. He was ready to take a drop of poison from his ring, because he was worried about being held captive, but suddenly a Turkish soldier cudgelled him on his back. "How dare you hit a nobleman?" the count said, whereby he got up, smacked him back with his horse whip, vaulted into the saddle, and left to rejoin his platoon.

> IN THOSE DAYS A NEW SPORT HAD BECOME TRENDY— SPEED SKATING, WHICH THE COUNT BECAME COMPLETELY HOOKED ON.

Although his fitness saved the count's life, he spent several months in a hospital bed in Bucharest. Ribeaupierre's military career ended after the Turkish attacks as he suffered from multiple war injuries. In spite of that, he was rewarded with the Order of St. Anna 4th Class for bravery in the Battle of Pleven (Plevno) in Bulgaria.

After his return to Saint Petersburg, the state of the count's health would not allow him to practise gymnastics again. Very soon he discovered something else—horses. In 1879, he built up a huge horse stable in town, including a covered racing track where races of trotters were held. He established two huge racing stables for thoroughbreds and stud horses at his estates in Kharkov and Simbirsk Guberny. He regularly held horse races on the best racing tracks there, where the top jockeys from both gubernies were present. Count Ribeaupierre was a club member of Emperor's Racing Association in Moscow and was also a master horseman to Tsar Alexander III.

In the 1890s, circles and clubs of heavy athletics—French wrestling, boxing and kettlebell exercises—started to appear in larger Russian towns. After the count had met Dr. Vladimir Krayewski and visited his circle of heavy athletics, he was thrilled by the muscular strongmen and the interesting training conducted by the old doctor himself. In the count's opinion, practice is second nature: "Don't be a theatregoer but an actor." He started to train on the mat and in the weight room. There is only one surviving report which shows his results. In the trunk-bend position he grabbed a kettlebell of two poods (32 kg), returned to a standing position, and three times performed a front raise parallel to the floor with that weight on his palm—that was an excellent performance for an amateur athlete.

The count paid for the term of the lease where the training of the wrestling club of Wladyslaw Pytlasinski was taking place, and on 30 January 1897 established The Saint Petersburg Athletic Association together with a prominent scientist, physiologist Peter F. Lesgaft.[2] Sections of athletics, gymnastics, acrobatics, wrestling, running, shooting and boxing were run under the leadership of the association. Ribeaupierre, as president and the main sponsor, was looking for athletes throughout the whole of Russia and enrolled them in championships in either Russia or abroad. He invited a boxing trainer, Ernesto Loustalot from France, who stayed in Russia and tutored in boxing (he also tutored writer Vladimir Nabokov).[3] At that time, the count entered into correspondence with a founder of the Olympic Movement, Baron Pierre de Coubertin, who invited the count to be a member of the International Olympic Committee.[4]

In 1900, a group of Russian athletes, who were chosen and sponsored by the count, went to Paris to the World Fair (Exposition Universelle), which was arranged concurrently with the Olympic Games. In 1908, on the eve of the Olympic Games in London, Ribeaupierre translated the Games programme into the Russian language and sent it to sports organizations to encourage a dignified representation of Russia. At the count's own expense, he sent three wrestlers to London, and two of them, Petrov and Orlov, brought home silver medals. The count initiated the foundation of the Russian Olympic Committee because of the high representation of Russian athletes at Olympic Games in 1912, in Stockholm.

The count gets enormous credit for the development of weightlifting and wrestling in Russia. There is a quote from David Webster's book *History of Weightlifting*: "On a cold February night in 1897, Dr. Krayewski and Count

> **IN THE COUNT'S OPINION, PRACTICE IS SECOND NATURE: "DON'T BE A THEATREGOER BUT AN ACTOR."**

> **"ON A COLD FEBRUARY NIGHT IN 1897, DR. KRAYEWSKI AND COUNT RIBEAUPIERRE TALKED ABOUT WEIGHTLIFTING AND THROUGH THEIR CONVERSATION DEVELOPED A BOLD PLAN."**

Ribeaupierre talked about weightlifting and through their conversation developed a bold plan. A few days later the news spread throughout the city. There would be a national weightlifting competition for the championship of Russia." From 15–26 April 1897, the first championship of Russia was held in Mikhailovskiy Arena, Saint Petersburg, and from then on, the glorious history of heavy athletics started to unfold in Russia.

As for the wrestling, the "belt style" was popular at that time in Russia, whilst the French style (now Greco–Roman wrestling) was known by hardly anybody. Ribeaupierre felt that the old Russian style was not good enough anymore, so he paid for the service of an experienced Polish wrestler, Wladyslaw Pytlasinski. The count, a sportsman to the core, had authority which stretched over European borders. Very soon all correspondence, including the news from foreign sports, went through his hands.

In 1902, he enrolled two wrestlers, Alex Aberg and Ivan Poddubny, at the World Wrestling Championships in Paris. Six months prior to the contest they were training in Saint Petersburg and eating their meals at a local inn, paid for by the count. Sergey Eliseyev and Georg Hackenschmidt also appreciated the count's generosity and support. In 1903, the weightlifter Eliseyev placed second at the World Championships in Paris, right behind the home team athlete Pierre Bonnes.

In 1898, all-rounder Hackenschmidt won the European Wrestling Championships in Vienna. Later on, he successfully wrestled in America and broke a number of records in weightlifting. The count also actively participated in the establishment of the Russian Weightlifting Association (1913) and co-organized the Second All-Russian Olympiad in Riga (1914).

There is one more quote from David Webster's book: [Sometime in 1898] "The arena of the riding school of Count Ribeaupierre was packed with the cream of Saint Petersburg society to watch a trial of strength between two of the count's horses and young Hackenschmidt. George was attempting the classic stunt of holding back two fine horses while grooms whipped the animals to make them pull with all their might. George Hackenschmidt easily mastered the horses amid thunderous cheers which grew even louder when he did a *lap of honour* round the arena carrying five of the count's grooms. The Tsar's uncle was there that day and presented the hero with a beautiful silver goblet."

Ribeaupierre in 1897.

Ribeaupierre (center with beard) on board the steamship Birma heading to the 1912 Olympic Games in London.

The old count (center) observing a race.

Boxer Ernest Loustalot.
Courtesy of Joseph Svub.

There is what Hack himself wrote in his book *The Way to Live*, published in 1908: [In February 1898] "Count Ribeaupierre took a keen interest in me and has continued to manifest his good will towards me ever since. He afterwards frequently supported and helped me, and I feel that I owe him a debt of gratitude."

According to IOC regulations, Ribeaupierre was chosen as a lifelong member of the organization; nevertheless, he resigned in 1913 due to his bad health. Baron Coubertin accepted his resignation. The Olympic cycle was interrupted during World War I, and Count Ribeaupierre, a great great-grandchild of a Russian warrior who captured Crimea, Prince Grigoriy A. Potemkin-Taurichesky, died of pneumonia on 4 June 1916 at home in Zykovsk Passage. The death of Georgiy Ivanovitch meant the end of the dynasty of Ribeaupierre in Russia; his name was lost and disappeared in revolution and civil war. His house and his arena in his riding school (including a hippodrome) were damaged, and they got rid of it during the reconstruction of the Belo-Russian Railroad. Nobody had visited his grave in Tsarskoye Selo.

These days the Historian–Sport museum is taking care of his grave and there is an exposition of documents, photographs, magazines and other items at Sirenevy Boulevard in memory of the patron of Russian heavy athletics, Count G. I. Ribeaupierre. **M**

Sources:

1. Magazines Sportivnaya zizn Rossii, No. 4/2006 & No. 10/2006.

Notes:

1. In comparison, the annual leave for a clerk of VIII Class and higher officers was roughly 450 roubles at that time. Whoever earned 100 roubles in a Russian village was "a fabulously wealthy man." In contrast, Prince G. A. Potemkin spent 200 thousand roubles for a festive suit.

2. Peter F. Lesgaft (1837–1909), an anatomist and a teacher, graduated from the Medical Surgical Academy (MSA) in 1861. Seven years later he became a professor of Kazan University. In 1871, he started teaching at the MSA. From 1874–1886, his primary interest was in the organisation of physical training in military educational institutions. From 1886–1897, he held teaching positions at the university in Saint Petersburg. In 1893, he established the biological laboratory, which was renamed the Lesgaft Institute of Natural Science in 1918. In 1896, Lesgaft initiated the courses of Female Teachers of Physical Education; in 1906–1907 the courses operated at the Pedagogical Department of the Higher Free School. In 1919, using these courses as the base, he set up the Lesgaft Institute of Physical Education (present-day Lesgaft Academy of Physical Culture).

3. Ernesto Loustalot was born in January 5, 1859, in Bordeaux, the son of a sailor. At 4 years of age, the boy began swimming lessons; at 5, boxing. Loustalot finished L'Ecole Militaire de l'éducation physique in Joinville-le-Pont (near Paris) with the gold medal and for eight years taught boxing, swimming, fencing and gymnastics there. He was the French gymnastics champion, the French and English boxing champion of Europe, and among the world's five best fencers. At the beginning of 1897, he was invited to teach sports at the Imperial School of Jurisprudence in Saint Petersburg. Loustalot did much for the popularisation and development of sports in Russia. He was the initiator of the first public boxing match that took place on 25 March 25 1898, in the Mikhailovskiy Arena in Saint Petersburg, where he boxed against his pupil, a certain Vains. He was among the first sportsmen to introduce the English and the French boxing styles in Russia where he trained several first-rate Russian boxers. He enjoyed great respect and popularity and became Russified with the years, so that a Russian patronymic was added to his name: Ernest Ivanovitch. After the revolution he refused to leave Russia, and from 1919 on, worked as a teacher of physical training and sports in the Higher School for Naval Officers at the famous Admiralty building. Loustalot died on 9 March 1931.

4. In 1894–1900, his predecessor was General Alexey de Boutowsky.

Physical Preparedness for PPP—And Anyone in Pursuit of Good Health

Ken Best

PPP stands for Public Protection Personnel. I use this term to describe the men and women employed to protect our public safety, prevent crime from flourishing, catch and detain criminals, and ensure that we as civilians can go about our business in relative peace. Public Protection Personnel include police officers, security personnel, corrections officers, local law enforcers, customs officials, and court officers (warrant officers and bounty hunters). They are the people we trust to carry out their duties in the pursuit of justice and for the preservation of the laws of society on a domestic level. Military personnel have similar goals, but because they are often employed overseas, they require a special level of strength and fitness that is beyond the scope of this article.

The duties of PPP are often active in nature and require members to possess a level of fitness and strength above that of the average person. Initial entry requirements have a physical component, and PPP recruits must pass a multitude of aerobic and strength tests if they are to gain employment in their chosen field. Once employed, officers may or may not have to maintain their fitness depending on their employment contract. Some employers insist their officers maintain fitness for safety reasons or for promotion to higher ranks; they may allow them to train during work hours or may offer to subsidize gym memberships and equipment costs. For many officers, however, this responsibility is left for them to attend to on their own time.

Ken Best on graduation day at the Queensland Police Academy on 1 July 1988. Photo by Patricia Robertson.

In either case, I firmly believe PPP should maintain a high degree of strength and fitness to meet the demands of their roles and to maximize on-the-job health and safety; however, experience has taught me that this is very hard to do. PPP duties have a lot of common elements that can negatively impact an officer's training program and motivation. Firstly, I'll present some of the more important ones and then suggest some ways you can manage them so that if you are a PPP member, you can maximize your training time and recovery. Most of the information in this article pertains to PPP employed to conduct the general duties of their position.

> PPP DUTIES HAVE A LOT OF COMMON ELEMENTS THAT CAN NEGATIVELY IMPACT AN OFFICER'S TRAINING PROGRAM AND MOTIVATION.

Officers who are in specialist teams such as SWAT, riot control, and dignitary protection will need more specific training programs (I recommend reading "Intensive Strength Training NSW-style for SWAT Units" by Sean Burns, MILO, June 2008, Vol. 16, No. 1 for an example of such a program).

PPP perform some sort of shift work. Officers usually work a three-shift roster that requires them to work mornings, evenings, and nights on set rotations. Some officers work different shifts on a weekly basis, and some work permanent late shifts. Shift work impacts the health and energy of the worker. Lack of sleep on shift work can occur on a regular basis and is sometimes unavoidable. Energy levels are constantly fluctuating and need to be managed if officers wish to maintain their training. Some officers travel a lot and could be away from familiar surroundings regularly and for long periods of time. Some are simply overrun with cases and work long hours to ensure all legal requirements, such as paperwork, are attended to. In a lot of PPP jobs, personnel work double shifts due to illness, injury, and constant lack of staff.

PPP are often required to control, transport and detain persons. Most PPP are entrusted to enforce a number of local, state and federal laws. In doing so, they often interact with the public in negative and volatile circumstances, leading to confrontation, conflict, and serious physical assault. Most PPP are working in unfamiliar environments in less-than-ideal conditions. They are required to make important and often life-altering decisions immediately while under duress, with no assistance or second chances. PPP can go from a sedentary, seated position to fighting for their lives in the blink of an eye. When it is time to act, they must act immediately, ethically, morally, lawfully, and with due consideration for the safety of themselves and others. They must use all their strength and conditioning to defend themselves when reasoning and negotiating fails.

Many PPP wear a uniform and carry heavy utilities such as radios, torches [flashlights], weapons, bullet-proof vests, packs, and heavy clothing and boots. They are often required to perform most of their duties with this equipment in tow, some of it weighing up to 40 kg. Whilst this weight may not sound heavy to strong MILO readers out there, try wearing a backpack with 40 kg in it and going about your business during the day (including training sessions) for eight or more hours. I can guarantee you'll be relieved at the end of the day to take off the pack, and you'll feel a deep tiredness in your muscles and a pounding headache. Now do it all again tomorrow, and the next night, and the next, and so on. You get the picture.

> . . . TRY WEARING A BACKPACK WITH 40 KG IN IT AND GOING ABOUT YOUR BUSINESS DURING THE DAY (INCLUDING TRAINING SESSIONS) FOR EIGHT OR MORE HOURS.

PPP often miss meals and work through meal breaks. Officers tend to make poor food choices because of time constraints or a lack of good food sources at odd hours. They also have trouble keeping hydrated unless they lug a bottle of water with them, and this is not always possible. They are at a higher risk of contracting infectious diseases and illnesses and suffer more workplace injuries than normal. Some injuries can cause serious bodily harm or death. PPP duties are very stressful, and place their personnel under constant pressure and risk. All these factors impact their general health and can cause serious down time in training and in life in general. Some officers succumb to alcohol and drug use to cope with their situation and to continue functioning. However, this is a dead-end street.

Strength training routines for PPP are often difficult to implement and sustain due to the above circumstances, as routines and schedules can be frequently interrupted. Nevertheless, if you are a PPP, you should do your utmost to train consistently on a well-planned routine of strength exercises. How you deal with these interruptions will make the difference between success and failure. You will need good time management skills and the ability to juggle schedules in order to fit in your workouts. Progress is possible but it will be up and down. Consistency boils down to attending to your workouts whenever possible and making gains in small amounts over the long haul. It will feel as if you are taking one step backward after every two steps forward, but at least you'll be moving in the right direction.

In my experience, a strength session should be a full-body workout consisting of compound exercises for the major muscle groups of the legs, shoulder girdle, and back. Use barbells and dumbbells for most of your exercises. Keep the weights moderately heavy and push the reps into the medium-to-high range: 10 for upper body and 20 for legs. Use a double-progression method where you increase the reps with the same weight until you reach the upper rep target and then add weight. The reason you do a whole-body session is that you cover all the major muscle groups in the time allotted because you don't know when you can return to training. Split routines are out of the question. Do what you can when you can, and return to the same routine in a few days' time.

The reason I recommend barbells and dumbbells over machines and other modes is because your work is ground-based in nature. You must rely on your physical preparedness for self-defense, searches, patrols, and people movements, and any number of other jobs that require good balance, coordination, and agility. Hopefully in situations such as these, your job-specific skills will kick in automatically, but you'll need functional strength and speed to back them up. In my experience, athletic strength movements performed with barbells and dumbbells are the best way to prepare your body for the types of demands placed on it by PPP duties.

> ALSO, YOUR TRAINING SHOULD PREPARE YOUR BODY TO GO FROM ZERO TO FULL-TILT IN A VERY SHORT TIME.

Also, your training should prepare your body to go from zero to full-tilt in a very short time. The best way to accomplish this with strength training is to reduce your warm-up sets to a minimum. Obviously, safety factors prevent you from jumping straight into your heavy sets straight away, but doing your heavy sets after one warm-up should be your goal. I don't recommend doing heavy, low-rep or single-rep strength training for PPP as this type of maximum strength isn't what you'll be using on the job. Therefore, doing one high-rep set before your work sets shouldn't put you in much danger of injury unless you already have one in the area of the body you're going to train. The Bulgarian weightlifters used this method successfully in the 1980s and they've showed no signs of slowing down since.

PPP should aim for good general health and circulation. Your body can tolerate extra demands placed on it from PPP work if it is fit and healthy. What this requires is attention to the other factors of good health: aerobic fitness, flexibility, rest, and a good diet. Perform aerobic training at least twice a week with an activity you enjoy. I prefer to do activities that cover the whole body in the session, such as swimming, rowing, heavy walking, bag work, and skipping. Once again, time is a factor, so do your aerobic sessions when you can, and try to go for at least half an hour. Interval sessions are good if you have less time than that on a particular day, but try to complete a longer session later in the week.

Rest and sleep are extremely important to PPP. Shift work, extended shifts, and overtime place great demands on your body. Scientific studies show that shift workers can reduce their lifespan by up to ten years if they do shift work their entire careers and don't take care of themselves. It really is that damaging if not managed properly. Lack of sleep for PPP can be fatal. If you're tired and stressed, your reaction times, decision-making skills, and observations will suffer, and according to Murphy's Law, they will falter just when you need them the most. To avoid becoming a victim of exhaustion, get as much rest and sleep as you can.

Try to get seven or more hours of sleep in a twenty-four hour period. I know from experience that this is nearly impossible when you are working through the night. Sleep in a darkened room with ear plugs in and try to air condition the room. The air conditioner will provide a comfortable environment to sleep in and some white noise to drown out other more annoying noises like lawnmowers, screaming children, vehicles, and loud music/TV. I found that getting the majority of sleep before my shift began helped me greatly. Most people sleep during the night, get up in the morning, have breakfast and go to work. By keeping this routine prior to a night shift, you are providing your brain with a familiar habit, thereby helping your body clock adjust more quickly to the altered wake-sleep cycle.

> LACK OF SLEEP FOR PPP CAN BE FATAL. IF YOU'RE TIRED AND STRESSED, YOUR REACTION TIMES, DECISION-MAKING SKILLS, AND OBSERVATIONS WILL SUFFER . . .

Flexibility is very important for PPP. Steve Jeck commented in his video "Of Stones and Strength" that you will get into some funky positions when lifting stones—and you will experience the same dilemma when performing PPP duties. You will get into situations that require doing one or more of the following: running, jumping, rolling on the ground, twisting, bending, and climbing and lifting objects and people from odd positions. Being flexible helps prevent injuries and helps your muscles to work at their full strength. Perform your stretches after aerobic and strength training. A stretching routine consisting of half a dozen movements held for 30 seconds each will do wonders for your well-being and recovery and won't take up much of your precious time.

Taking into consideration the above information, an example of a good, all-round strength training routine would look like this:

Dumbbell or kettlebell swings	2 x 20 (first set with 16 kg, second with 24 kg)
Squats	1 x 10, 1 x 20 (back, front or hip-belt)
Dips	b/w x 10, 2 x 8 (weighted)
Pull-ups	b/w x 10, 2 x 5 (weighted, with underhand or parallel grip)
Dumbbell presses	1 x 10, 1 x 6
Farmer's walk with heavy dumbbells	2 x 50 m

Ab/core, neck and extra grip work of your choice

Attempt this routine at least twice a week. If you have the time and energy, do it three times a week, but always follow a heavy session with a light one. Don't train fewer than three times every two weeks; otherwise your strength and conditioning will start to wane.

If you find that you can't return to the weights for six or seven days because of work commitments, try to fit in a quick session of high-rep bodyweight squats, sit-ups, push-ups, and neck and grip work on day three or four to maintain your strength. When you get back to the weights routine, start with the same weights you trained with last time and increase from there. Don't forget to stretch, do your cardio, eat well and sleep as much as possible. As you progress in your training, you'll notice the benefits will carry over to your work performance.

Physical preparedness is not something you should ignore if you are going to perform PPP work. Even if you hold a non-operational position or support role, you should pay attention to your fitness, health and strength—just in case. You never know, you could get called back to duty anytime; or you could be off-duty and need your physical skills to help yourself or someone in need.

And besides, good health is priceless. Paying attention to a progressive training routine, good nutrition, and sound sleep is never a waste of time. Good health really is the only fountain of youth in existence, and will not only enhance your working life but your life at play as well. And remember, be safe out there! M

> GOOD HEALTH REALLY IS THE ONLY FOUNTAIN OF YOUTH IN EXISTENCE . . .

IRON FILINGS

Randall J. Strossen, Ph.D. | *Publisher & Editor-in-chief*

GNC and the Gillinghams have been acting as goodwill ambassadors to the U.S. military. "Several times a year GNC sends one of the Gillingham brothers to special events at military base GNC stores," Wade Gillingham told us.

"This is part of GNC's promotional efforts to support our nation's armed services. The events include autograph signing, free samples, and drawings or competitions to win prize packages. Today I was at Warren Air Force Base in Cheyenne, Wyoming, for a grand reopening of the GNC store. We ran a grip challenge using IronMind's Captains of Crush Grippers, with the individual who closed the hardest gripper for the most reps winning a GNC Backpack loaded with products. Our top effort was one rep with the No. 1.5."

"The military stores are a top priority for GNC," said Karl Gillingham. "Each year, [brothers] Brad, Wade, and I do multiple appearances at military branches across the country to promote GNC, support the troops, and answer training and supplementation questions. It is a great program, especially in times of conflict like we have now. Today I was at Fort Rucker in Alabama. They had their base powerlifting championships, and I went over to show support for the contest and to do a grand reopening of the GNC on base. I met and talked to several helicopter pilots who are heading for the front lines. I thanked them for their courage and call of duty to our country. Military personal are ultimately top athletes, and anything I can do to help their performance and spirit is good for our freedom fighters." M

Best known for his Olympic-style weightlifting career, David Morgan gave the CrossFit King Kong workout a try, just to see how he'd stack up on the strength–endurance challenge involving cycles of deadlifts, muscle-ups, cleans, and handstand press-ups. Morgan, for the record, is 44, so he's something of a senior citizen in the crowd of super-fitsters, but no matter, he figured. Showing his confidence, instead of using the standard of 255 lb. for the clean and 455 lb. for the deadlift, Morgan upped the ante to 275 lb./500 lb., respectively.

Facing a record time of 2:31.47, Morgan ran through the workout in a mere 2:04 and later told IronMind, "I could have done it with 300 lb. and 600 lb." Morgan, who is quick to commend the difficulty of this CrossFit challenge given its demands to be both strong and fit, is no ordinary trainee: besides being a five-time Commonwealth Games gold medalist in weightlifting and a two-time Olympian in the sport, Morgan's good at a handful of other lifts and has a history of taking on and succeeding at a range of physical challenges.

Rather than idling away his Saturday chasing cats or taking a nap, Tater headed to Cotati, in Northern California's world famous wine country, for the Redwood Empire Open Weightlifting Championships—where a good time was had by all.
Randall J. Strossen photo.

Unlike some strength sports, wine instead of whine was the order of the day at the Redwood Empire Open Weightlifting Championships in Sonoma Country, California. Limited to 60 competitors, the Redwood Empire Open drew lifters from across the board—young, not so young; men and women; novice and experts, alike. At the expert end, lifters included Ian Wilson, the 15-year old who is making waves in the weightlifting world, and Donnie Shankle, a top American weightlifter in the 105-kg category.

Hosted by Myles Ahead Fitness and set in Cotati, California's La Plaza Park, this meet showed how much fun Olympic weightlifting can be . . . a winning combination of dogs, beer, wine, BBQ, and Olympic weightlifting in the park.

Back about 10 years or so, IronMind ran a little contest in *MILO*, asking readers to name the three people who had lifted the Inver Stone overhead. A few came up with Bill Kazmaier and Francis Brebner, but Hamish Davidson, the elusive third, was unnamed. Since that time, the field has doubled.

Stone lifting aficionado and lifting history buff Roger Davis wrote to IronMind, "Firstly, congratulations to Andy Cairney on his magnificent press of the Inver Stone—he made it look easy . . . Just to let you know, Andy is in fact the sixth person to have pressed the Inver, not the fourth," continued Davis, supplying the following list of those who have succeeded in getting the Inver Stone overhead:

1. Bill Kazmaier
2. Hamish Davidson
3. Francis Brebner
4. Laine Snook
5. Sebastian Wenta
6. Andy Cairney

You might hang on to this list, just in case we decide to run a contest again.

When this subject came up several years ago at a World's Strongest Man contest, Bill Kazmaier—the man who dropped jaws by being the first man to lift overhead the stone that many others would have been happy to hoist waist high—was nonchalant about his performance. Nodding toward a group of World's Strongest Man competitors, the Kaz told Randall Strossen, "Any of these guys could do it."

The Inver Stone at rest.
Randall J. Strossen photo.

If you want to be up on the action, follow IronMind on Twitter for breaking news and interesting strength-world tidbits. If you can't get enough IronMind news and would also like easy access to the latest in the strength world, daily tweets from IronMind will keep you informed about what's going on. IronMind sent up-to-the-minute tweets from the field at Fortissimus and at the 2009 IHGF World Championships in Scotland, for example, and from World's Strongest Man in Malta. **M**

Olympic bobsled hopeful Ingrid Marcum headed to Lake Placid in the fall after a tour in Calgary, Alberta (Canada) for push training and testing. "I pushed well, placing fourth in the Push Championships—just .03 seconds out of third . . . I did well enough to keep myself in the mix."

Ingrid Marcum played a key role in the IronMind Invitational that brought the German Men's Olympic Weightlifting Team—featuring Olympic gold medalist Matthias Steiner—to the main stage of the Expo Hall at the Arnold Sports Festival earlier this year. As a dramatic counterpoint to the German men, Ingrid helped make the show that counted California Governor Arnold Schwarzenegger among its spectators.

In June, Ingrid won the USA Weightlifting National Championships in the 75-kg class and later that month she worked with John Brookfield on a training video featuring his Battling Ropes training system. "I have really enjoyed working with John, and filming the DVD this summer, and have incorporated the ropes into my own training!" said Ingrid.

Back to weightlifting and the qualifiers for the team going to the 2009 World

James Cook photo.

Courtesy of Ingrid Marcum.

"The fastest track in the world is the new 2010 Olympic track in Whistler," Ingrid Marcum told us. "The women's sleds were approaching 90 mph, and the men's 4-man sleds were approaching 95 mph! Most tracks are a little slower, with the women sliding at 75–80. I was with the world team in Whistler last season, and that track is definitely quick! Park City, which is normally considered a faster track, felt much slower after returning from Whistler."

Weightlifting Championships, Ingrid said that she would "love to be out there competing, [but] I had too much going on with the bobsled."

"We will be in Lake Placid . . . after which we will travel to Park City. There will be two races on each track before the U.S. National team is named in late October. Overall, the U.S. brakemen are very strong and very fast this season, so competition is fierce! . . . [I'm] looking forward to the competitive season, though we still have a long road ahead." M

Just to give you an idea of the variety of strength contests going on this past summer, here is a brief look at several from around the world, one Highland Games, one strongman, and one combo, known as Highlander.

North American Highlander Association
Reported by Thomas Van Vleck

There's a new organization called the North American Highlander Association. Highlander combines strongman and the heavy events from Scottish Highland Games, and the NAHA is a group that is trying to promote that concept with a very simple premise: have a meet with an equal number of strongman events and heavy events.

The first-ever NAHA Highlander event was the Jackson Weightlifting Club (JWC) Highlander, which also served as the Missouri State Championships. Held in Kirksville, Missouri, on June 13, 2009, it included the continental clean, stone lifting, and the farmer's walk from the strongman side; and the weight-over-bar, sheaf toss, and heavy hammer from the heavy events side; and it featured some great throwing and lifting by top athletes from both sports.

Viking Strength Highlander Challenge was held July 11, 2009 in Conroe, Texas, featuring some of the best that strongman has to offer. Guys like Jim Glassman, who has been on top for many years, and the Vincent brothers put a lively face on this meet. Matthew Vincent got the most attention from the audience, not only for throwing the light weight for distance over 70', but for being a real Highland Games guy and not wearing anything under his kilt. His brother Andy Vincent got in a monster throw with the 25-lb. stone and got 39'.

In the deadlift, Ryan Bracewell was the king and smoked 725 lb. raw, and lifted 800 lb. above his knees, but could not lock out. The press medley included a 174-lb. Inch replica dumbbell and Andy Vincent smoked all three in only 17 seconds. Travis Ortmayer was on hand and wanted to jump in and throw the weights around—Travis gave away the trophies and showed his support for Highlander competitions.

Ryan Bracewell deadlifting 725 lb. raw at the Viking Strength Highlander in Conroe, Texas.
Photo courtesy Svavar Sigursteinsson.

Dino Gym Highlander was held July 18, 2009 at the legendary Dino Gym in Holland, Kansas (I dare you to find it on a map). Scott Tully put on the meet with help of Al Myers. The middleweight division was extremely competitive, with only 3 points separating first from fourth. Chad Ullom tied Ryan Batchman but got the win due to the tiebreaker.

The 1st Annual Nebraska Highlander was held on August 15, 2009 by NAHA president D. J. Satterfield. There were competitors from all strength and sports avenues: Highland Games, strongman, powerlifting, arena football, and more. Sean Betz, pro world champion in Highland Games, won all three heavy events, and came in third place overall. M

WSM Super Series in Bucharest: A Win for Marshall White
Reported by Kjell Karlsson

Rarely has a strongman competition been as dramatic to the very end as when Marshall White (USA) took home the victory in the first WSM Super Series competition of the year. It was neck and neck right up into the very last event—the Atlas stones. On 4 July it was finally time for the much-awaited premiere of this year's WSM Super Series.

There was a great deal of interest from Sweden in Johannes Årsjö, a 23-year-old who has had a steeply rising career up to the ranks of the world's best. What could he possibly achieve against such established names as Janne Virtanen, Stojan Todorchev, and Brian Shaw, or any of the other four Americans, including Nick Best and Marshall White, who had travelled to Bucharest, Romania?

As early as the first event, Apollon's Axle, Johannes demonstrated that he was prepared to fight, with a second place win after victor Brian Shaw, who lifted 186 kg. In the next event, winner Marshall White looked like a true Viking, carrying the Husafell Stone 83.8 m. Second was his countryman Nick Best, and third was Johannes Årsjö, who became the overall leader as a result. Fastest in the Farmer's Walk was Stojan Todorchev with a time of 12 seconds flat, closely followed by Nick Best, who then took the lead overall.

Rain started to fall over Bucharest, which didn't make it any easier for the athletes. Event four was the Super Yoke, weighing 410 kg for 20 m on the clock, and Nick Best went the distance in 8.88 seconds; shortly after came Stojan Todorchev in 9.07 seconds, an impressive time for an amateur.

Nick Best was still at the top coming into the final two events, and it was now time to cut the line-up. The scores were changed as well, which meant that the difference between the finalists were halved, and we got to see a really tight scoreboard. Going into the final events were Nick Best in the lead, Brian Shaw, Johannes Årsjö (now third), Stojan Todorchev, Marshall White, and Janne Virtanen.

The Crucifix Hold of two Viking swords at arms' length for as long as possible was the next event. Janne Virtanen took his first event victory with a time of 38.84 seconds, closely followed by Marshall White and Johannes Årsjö.

Going into the final event, the Atlas Stones, Johannes was again leading the competition—albeit by 0.25 points and with the top five contestants within 1.25 points. Not even Alfred Hitchcock could have directed a more exciting finish!

The Atlas stones would decide the entire competition—that much was clear. Janne Virtanen was first, putting four stones in place. Brian put the fifth in place with a time of 38.94 seconds. Stojan Todorchev managed only four stones in a fast 16.95 seconds and might have gone at it a little too hard. Nick Best was the second to lift all five stones and he did it in 35.78 seconds, taking over the lead. Marshall White now had the chance to pass him, which he did with a terrific time of 28.5 seconds. Last out was Johannes Årsjö. Would he manage all five stones and be able to beat White's phenomenal 28.5 seconds? The answer to the first question was yes! . . . and the answer to the second question was no. With a time of 37.69 seconds, Årsjö squeezed between Nick Best and Brian Shaw, into third place.

The standard of competition in Bucharest was high throughout, and the outcome shows that strongman is definitely a spectator sport at its best.

Final results
1.	Marshall White	28.5
2.	Nick Best	27
3.	Johannes Årsjö	26.75
4.	Brian Shaw	24.5
5.	Stojan Todorchev	23.5
6.	Janne Virtanen	19.5

M

IHGF World Highland Games Team Championships
Reported by Francis Brebner

Antigonish, Canada was the host of this year's inaugural IHGF World Highland Games Team Championships. From the moment the athletes arrived until the time of their departure, their stay was well-planned and coordinated. Four records tumbled over the two days, and the highlight was when Mike Zolkiewicz set a new world record in the 56-lb. weight-for-height at 18' 9"!

In the first event, the 22-lb. Braemar stone, Sean Betz established a new ground record with a distance of 41' 7-1/2", breaking the old record of 40' 5" held by Matt Docherty. In the 56-lb. weight-for-distance, Greg Hadley smashed his own Canadian record of 45' 7" with a tremendous throw of 46'. The 22-lb. hammer was a very exciting contest, with Lyle Barron taking the win with a world-class throw of 112' 5-3/4".

Next up was the caber toss with a pole weighing 123-lb. and 21' 8" in length with very little taper, and first place went to Brock with a toss of 11:00.

The final event of the first day's competition, the 56-lb. weight-for-height, proved riveting for the six thousand spectators, who watched Zolkiewicz win the event at a very impressive height of 17'. The excitement did not end there as Zolkiewicz asked for the bar to be raised to the new height of 18' 9", which was 1' 3" higher than the existing Antigonish ground record, held by Holland's Wout Zjilstra since 2003, and 1" higher than the existing world record of 18' 8", also held by Wout Zjilstra.

With the crowd encouraging him, Mike's first three attempts just narrowly missed clearing the bar. With three more record attempts, Zolkiewicz nailed the second one, establishing the new world record height of 18' 9" to the wild cheers of the crowd.

Day two got off to a strong start for Canadian Matt Docherty, who won the 16-lb. open stone with a putt of 52' 7". In the 28-lb. weight-for-distance, yet another ground record bit the dust. The large crowd of Highland Games fans cheered on Larry Brock as he blasted out a throw of 86' 6", which obliterated the old record of 86'.

The final scoring event of the championships, the 16-lb. hammer, proved a real ding-dong battle between Betz, Brock, and Lyle Barron, with Barron coming out on top with the winning distance of 132' 10-1/2".

The overall results were as follows:

USA Team 2 – Larry Brock and Mike Zolkiewicz	67
USA Team 1 – Sean Betz and Will Barron	73
Canada Team 2 – Lyle Barron and Derek Bishop	77
Canada Team 1 – Greg Hadley and Matt Docherty	92.5
Europe Team – Craig Sinclair and Tommy DeBruijn	125.5

M

Who's New

We've added three formidable gripsters to our No. 3 Captains of Crush Grippers certified list:

Jonathan Vogt
Taichi Morodomi
Timo Tuukkanen

For a complete list of those certified on the No. 3, No. 3.5, and No. 4 Captains of Crush Grippers, or for the Rules for Closing and Certification, please visit the IronMind website at
www.ironmind.com.

Jonathan Vogt proved he has world-class grip strength, and if that's not enough, he also helped out Jesse Marunde's children.
Photo courtesy of Jonathan Vogt.

IronMind is proud to contribute $500 to the educational trust funds for Jesse Marunde's children in honor of teenager Jonathan Vogt's mighty accomplishment of closing the No. 3 Captains of Crush Gripper. Jonathan, of Columbus, Indiana, is 19 years old, 6' 1", and weighs 240 lb.

Jonathan has his own landscaping business, which is helping to put him through school at Purdue University. Of his "hands being ready for the heavier grippers," he gives a lot of credit to his "gear-drive walk-behind Scag Mower—it is driven from the gear box to belts, which are tensioned with two springs that my hands have to pull up to turn." Jonathan has recently started competing in armwrestling tournaments and thinks that "the best thing to increase your hand strength on the [Captains of Crush] Grippers are holds with a heavy gripper." Congratulations, Jonathan! M

Taichi Morodomi, of Fukuoka, Japan, is 28 years old and 172 cm (5' 8") tall, and weighs 100 kg (220 lb.). Taichi has been training for 10 years, but only started his grip training a little over a year ago, with the specific goal "to try IronMind's certificate attempt." Taichi credits a healthy diet and balanced meals as well as single-rep pyramid training with helping him conquer this feat of hand strength. Taichi works in the restaurant business, and also enjoys lure fishing, drawing, and blogging.

His future goals are to master the No. 3.5 Captains of Crush Gripper as well as the IronMind Red Nail.

Well done, Taichi! M

Taichi Morodomi.
Photo courtesy of Keiko Kawaguchi/Iron Man Japan.

Timo Tuukkanen. Photo courtesy of Timo Tuukkanen.

Timo Tuukkanen is a 30-year-old grip enthusiast from Kotka, Finland, who is 188 cm (6' 2") tall and weighs 120 kg (265 lb.). Timo has been training his grip now for almost a year: "Since my grip progress has been quite nice—[either] by nature or as a result of my physical work with conveyor belts installation at our family-owned company—I don't have any other options than focus on certifying [on the] No. 3.5 in the future! I have focused on other grip strength methods also like the Rolling Thunder, Apollon's Axle, blocks, pinching, etc."

Also, Timo found that he is well-suited to the 200-kg steelcase timed holds [like a farmer's walk], setting two new Finnish records: 28 sec. right hand and 37 sec. right and left hands at the Fitness Expo. "Also I have held for time a 250-kg steelcase 2 sec., also a Fininsh record."

Timo would like to thank his training buddy, Juha Harju, who "has given me golden tips and tricks for grip training." Way to go, Timo! M

Overtraining:
What It Is and How to Avoid It

Jim Schmitz
U.S. Olympic Team Weightlifting Coach 1980, 1988, & 1992

When athletes begin weightlifting, they have no idea of what overtraining is—they just want to get as big and strong as possible as soon as they can, and they always want to stay at the highest level possible. Sooner or later, though, everyone learns about overtraining.

What is overtraining—signs and symptoms

Scientifically speaking, "overtraining is a consequence of imbalance between stress and adaptability of the body." (Mel Siff, *Supertraining*) I'm no sports scientist, physiologist, or kinesiologist, but I have read their articles and books on overtraining and, believe me, there are volumes on the subject and it can get quite complicated. I will try to make overtraining as understandable as possible.

> IT CAN BE THE RESULT OF NOT ENOUGH REST FOR RECOVERY, OR JUST GOING TOO HARD AND TOO HEAVY FOR TOO OFTEN AND TOO LONG.

Overtraining is a physical and/or a psychological condition that happens to you when you are on a prolonged high-intensity and/or high-volume training routine. It is where you are tired, sore, slow, uncoordinated, or unmotivated, and your results have stagnated or even regressed. It can be the result of not enough rest for recovery, or just going too hard and too heavy for too often and too long. However, it is not to be confused with being out of shape, when you are training harder than you are in condition to do.

Overtraining can manifest itself as any one, or incredibly all, of these symptoms:

1. You are always tired and it takes you longer to complete your workout
2. Your body, including muscles and joints, is sore all over
3. Your light and medium weights feel very heavy
4. You just can't seem to move as fast as you normally can

5. Your coordination isn't as good as normal
6. You just aren't motivated and you dread going to the gym
7. You have several small injuries

Early in my career when I began getting stronger, I wanted to be able to power clean 300 lb. (136 kg) and back squat 500 lb. (227 kg) anytime and anywhere because I had a guy training in my gym, Chet Pape, who could do that. Chet was a 198-lb. (90-kg) lifter in the San Francisco Bay Area in the 1960s and 1970s whose best clean and jerk was 340 lb. (154.5 kg) and best back squat was 550 lb. (250 kg). However, for at least 10 years he could power clean 300 lb. and back squat 500 lb. anytime, anywhere—he was very strong. For some reason he felt he had to do those weights or there was something wrong with him.

Naturally, several of us wanted to be not just strong, but strong like Chet, "Mr. 300 and 500 anytime, anywhere." Well, I (and a few others) eventually did do the 300-lb. power clean and 500-lb. back squat on several occasions, but that is where I really learned about overtraining. You see, for Chet, 300 lb. and 500 lb. was 80 to 90%; for me and the others, it was plus 100%. When I finally attained those lifts, I was able to do them twice in one week, then once a week, then not at all. I was sore and tired, and the weights seemed to be getting heavier and I, weaker. What was going on?

Balancing your workout intensity and volume

I had learned firsthand about overtraining and began to learn about how to avoid it. You avoid it by not going to your maximum too often and by balancing your workout's intensity and volume. However, that is both a science and an art, because how do you train hard enough to make gains, but not so hard as to overtrain? A line from the great U.S. coach Joe Mills (coach of Bob Bednarski and Mark Cameron) applies here. Joe said, "I can tell you all I know about weightlifting in forty-five minutes, but it will take you a lifetime to understand it."

This is why cycling, peaking, and periodization training methods were developed. These three terms all refer to the same principle of planning one's training for maximum progress without overtraining or getting injured. *Cycling* refers to repeating your training programs on a scheduled recurring sequence. *Peaking* refers to increasing your training intensity so that you will be in your top physical and psychological condition for an event where you want to have your very best performance. *Periodization* combines peaking and cycling to form a training plan that will get the best results without overtraining. In other words, you cycle your workouts in order to peak for competition or goals, and you do this for a period of time. For example, one period might be 12 weeks where you are concentrating on building up your leg strength. Then you might follow that period with 8 weeks of improving your snatch and clean and jerk. The following chart is a general example of a 12- and 8-week cycle. You can refer to my *MILO* article, "Cycling, Peaking, and Periodization" [June 2006, Vol. 14, No. 1] for more information on cycling, peaking, and periodization.

Cycles, peaks, and periodization

<u>12-week cycle</u>
week 1 – 60%, week 2 – 70%, week 3 – 80%, week 4 – 90%,
week 5 – 65%, week 6 – 75%, week 7 – 85%, week 8 – 95%,
week 9 – 70%, week 10 – 80%, week 11 – 90%, week 12 – 100%

Cycles, peaks, and periodization

8-week cycle
week 1 – 70%, week 2 – 80%, week 3 – 90%, week 4 – 95%, week 5 – 75%, week 6 – 85%, week 7 – 95%, week 8 – 100%

Training hard and making gains— and backing off

Therein lies the dilemma— how do you get as strong and as powerful as possible without overtraining or getting injured? Also, what about when everything is just going great and you are making progress and PRs at almost every workout? We've all been there when our training conditions are just right; we have time to train as hard as we can; we have time to rest, sleep and recover, and time and money to eat as we should; our job or school is under control; and our family and social life are all fine, with no undue stress. That's when you can devote all the energy and focus necessary for training hard and making the big gains. It is during these times that we make great gains; but if we aren't careful, we will also overtrain. And if we are really tough, as almost all of us are, we will try to push through these hard, tough workouts, and eventually we'll crash—either by getting injured or becoming mentally burned-out and even unable to get out of bed!

If you train yourself, you are more susceptible to overtraining. The other common factor in overtraining is the overenthusiastic and inexperienced coach. I've been guilty of both. I was coaching a young and very talented lifter by the name of John Bergman, super heavyweight from 1981 to 1988. John became a national junior champion; placed fifth at the 1982 Junior World Championships; was a senior national champion in 1986; placed second to his training partner, Mario Martinez, in the 1987 Pan American Games; and placed tenth in the 1988 Olympics. In 1987 John's best lifts were 180 kg and 215 kg in a local competition. He had a training PR clean and jerk of 225 kg. We thought he was on his way— but that was the mountain top.

> THEREIN LIES THE DILEMMA— HOW TO GET AS STRONG AND AS POWERFUL AS POSSIBLE WITHOUT OVERTRAINING OR GETTING INJURED?

He had been making tremendous gains that year and I didn't want to slow him down or back him off—that was a big mistake. He didn't have any major injuries, but numerous little ones—knee, hip, shoulder, and wrist strains that prevented doing the 180-kg and 225-kg lifts again. We would back off until he healed up completely and then start back training hard and heavy. He could do 170 and 200 with no problem, but getting to the next level always brought back the nagging little injuries. It was very frustrating for both of us. He struggled in 1987 and 1988 and competed in the Olympics, doing only 167.5 and 185 kg. I always wonder how his career would have been if I had backed off his training in that winter of 1987.

When backing someone off heavy training, you might wonder, how far do you back off? This is where science and art have to work together. Our bodies aren't machines and therefore can't follow set programs designed by

> As a coach, you really should be very knowledgeable in the science and theory of training, but you must always remember you are training humans.

scientists or by computers. As a coach, you really should be very knowledgeable in the science and theory of training, but you must always remember you are training humans. Humans have situations and problems that affect training, like work, school, and family, and there are emotional and psychological factors as well.

Preventing overtraining with balanced workouts

That is the million dollar question: "How do you prevent overtraining?" First, you have to get yourself in condition for hard, heavy training by building up your workout capacity, which is the ability to do several lifts in a workout for many sets and reps. You build up your volume of sets and reps, but not with your heaviest weights. You then change your program to heavier weights for fewer sets and reps. Doing a balanced workout is of first importance.

That raises the question, what is a balanced workout? Simply put, it is one that takes about an hour and a half to two hours with a warm-up; stretching; heavy, medium, and light lifting; and a taper-off or cool-down period. After your warm-up, you do what you want to emphasize most in that workout. See the chart below for a balanced workout profile. Also, check my articles on program design, "Ordering Up Results" [MILO, December 1998, Vol. 6, No. 3] and "Training Programs" [MILO, September 2006, Vol. 13, No. 2].

You must always balance your workouts with what you want to accomplish and where you are in your training cycle. Whether you are an intermediate lifter or Olympic champion, you must have a training plan and follow cycles or periods of different training levels and lifts if you want to avoid overtraining. The number one priority is to have a proper training plan, including methods, cycles, peaks, and periods.

Balanced workouts

Workout A	Workout B	Workout C
Heavy/medium	Heavy/light	Heavy/heavy
Warm-up	Warm-up	Warm-up
Back squat – heavy	Jerk – heavy	Snatch – heavy
Power snatch – medium	Hang snatch – light	Clean and jerk – heavy
Power clean – medium	Hang clean – light	Clean pull – heavy
Snatch high pull – medium	Overhead squat – medium	Front squat – medium
Push jerk – light	Military press – light	Push press – light

Rest and recovery

Next, you must get enough rest for recovery. That means 7 to 9 hours sleep a night and maybe an hour or so nap during the day, if you can. You must eat enough and correctly. If you want your body to perform at a high level, you must supply it with high-quality food or fuel. Proper nutrition is necessary for energy for your workouts and for tissue repair and tissue-building after your workouts. When I started out, the rule of thumb for nutrition was to eat as much as possible and let your body sort out what it needed. Proper nutrition for athletes has come a long way since then.

You also need to keep mentally as stress free as possible. Stress drains your energy and distracts your concentration. I like what Bob Hoffman used to say: "You need to keep a tranquil mind."

> I LIKE WHAT BOB HOFFMAN USED TO SAY: "YOU NEED TO KEEP A TRANQUIL MIND."

Saunas and massages are great for recovery. The best weightlifting countries in the world always have a masseur as part of their team, and they are the hardest workers on the team, giving every lifter several massages a day. If you were around during the 1970s and 1980s and saw the Soviet team in Gettysburg for the 1978 Worlds or in Las Vegas for the Record Makers event, you saw (and maybe met) Genadi Baldin. Genadi was the Soviet team masseur for about 15 years before the president of Russia, Boris Yeltsin, stole him away for his personal service.

If you don't have access to a masseur and/or a sauna, try the hot and cold shower routine: take as hot a shower as you can stand for several minutes, and then switch to as cold as you can handle for a few minutes; then repeat hot, cold, hot, and cold—about 20 minutes total time should be enough. The theory here is that you are flushing the waste products and lactic acid (the substances that give you sore muscles) out of your tissues and body by having the blood rush to the skin under hot water and then back to the tissues and muscles under cold water. It really does seem to work, but it is tough to do. It doesn't feel good when you are doing it, but it sure feels good afterward.

Light workouts are necessary, sometimes for a week or two or even longer. I know some feel that if they are going to train light, it's not worth going to the gym and it is better to just stay home and rest, but believe it or not, light workouts speed up recovery. You must make sure it is a really light workout, 50-60% tops, and don't go crazy on the reps just because you're using very light weights. Taking a break from lifting weights works too, but you lose technique and conditioning and you have to start back light anyway; so just train light until you feel rejuvenated. This way you will come back faster and maybe better.

If you feel you absolutely must take time off from the weights, don't let yourself get completely out of shape. At least do some stretching, preferably a little every day, and it is always a good idea to do some stomach work every day as well. Doing other physical activities, like swimming, jogging, and playing sports like baseball, basketball, soccer, volleyball, or tennis, is also very good. Participate in your other sports for fun and relaxation, but don't injure yourself being a weekend warrior while you are recovering from overtraining.

Proper nutrition

Proper nutrition will help prevent overtraining and enhance recovery. We have learned so much about nutrition for athletes over the last 49 years (when I first began training) when we thought proper nutrition was just eating a lot. Become a student of nutrition—read and study it as much as you can, because proper nutrition not only will enhance your athletic career, but also will help you lead a long, healthy life after your high-performance sports days are over. Don't get caught up in fads and trends; remember, if it sounds too good to be true, it *is* too good to be true! Vitamins and supplements are good and do work, but I just want to give you a very big warning here: be careful! Good food is the best. You can't replace good natural food with vitamins and supplements; they are meant to add to your nutritional requirements, not replace them.

It's very common to overtrain when one is preparing for the biggest event of his year or her career. I've seen many a top lifter do much less in competition than he did in training just a week or so before. I'm often telling my lifters that we want to do it in competition, not in the gym—you don't get any medals or records in the gym. You've got to train as hard as you possibly can, but not leave it in the gym. That's why I back my lifters off their training intensity considerably about 7 days before a competition. I'd rather have my lifter compete slightly undertrained than overtrained.

> I JUST WONDER, IF HE HADN'T TRAINED SO HARD THE WEEK BEFORE, COULD HE HAVE MADE THE WINNING LIFTS?

If you have seen the IronMind Training Hall video of Stefan Botev (Bulgaria and Australia) at the 1995 World Championships, you saw him try a 200-kg snatch and 250-kg clean and jerk many, many times in one incredible training session less than a week before his competition. He had at least 3 misses with each. It looked as if he were just beating himself up. The winning total that year was 442.5 kg, second was 440, and Botev was third with 435. I just wonder, if he hadn't trained so hard the week before, could he have made the winning lifts?

Train as hard as you possibly can, but just as you can't drive your car at maximum RPMs and speed all the time, neither can you push your body to its max all the time. I tell people that training is a lot like driving a car—you step on the gas and back off the gas, and you'll last longer and go farther. Also, like a car, your body has to be well-maintained, nurtured, and cared for at the highest level. Treat your body like an Indianapolis 500 race car. Give it the best fuel (food), service (training methods), and driver (coach) you possibly can and you will achieve your highest and best results possible. **M**

> I'D RATHER HAVE MY LIFTER COMPETE SLIGHTLY UNDERTRAINED THAN OVERTRAINED.

The Art and Science of Recovery

Brian Mangravite

There has been a great deal of discussion, controversy, and outright argument about the appropriate level and kind of stress to impose on a body to elicit growth. Equally as contentious has been the related topic of recovery. The only thing that has been agreed upon is that some kind of stress is required followed by some kind of recovery. Everything else to do with training has had as many proponents as there are trainees. Everyone has an opinion. Most of them have one basic flaw: almost every athlete overestimates his ability to recover.

I must say up front that I am fully aware that many sports require a high volume of training because there is a skill component that demands a great deal of training, i.e., practice. I remember reading a statistic somewhere that said that to reach elite status in any given sport required, absolutely *required*, about 15,000 hours of training. It takes that long to condition the nervous system, develop the muscular coordination and reaction time, and master the skill sets to be an elite athlete in a given sport. In case you haven't done the math, that works out to about 6 hours a day, 7 days a week for seven years. Doing fewer hours a day or taking layoffs here and there, you'd have to keep at it for more than seven years—it's that simple. Now you know why so few individuals can truly excel in more than one sport.

For the purposes of building raw strength and power, most people still train too long or too often or both. One simple fact is that your ability to recover from a workout is largely genetic and highly variable from person to person, and it doesn't change much with greater conditioning. Consequently, you may be capable of a good deal more work as you become more advanced, but your ability to recover from that work improves only slightly, if at all. Thus, you are more likely to overtrain as an advanced trainer than you are as a beginner. Maybe this is why gains seem to come so easily when one first starts training, and then the gains come more and more slowly as one advances. Progress is bound to slow eventually as you approach what could be called your "genetic maximum strength"—the

> NOW YOU KNOW WHY SO FEW INDIVIDUALS CAN TRULY EXCEL IN MORE THAN ONE SPORT.

strongest you could ever be based on your genetics—but that maximum is much higher than most people will ever achieve.

The first thing is to not change training frequency as you become more advanced. In fact, due to your increased workload ability, you'd probably make better progress by decreasing frequency as you progress. I remember when I was a teenager first starting out in lifting, the standard was to work out three times a week. I made decent progress with that schedule. Then my older brother found that he actually did better training twice a week. I tried it—he was right. Then I got bit square in the ass by the iron bug when I hit college and started training six days a week . . . and progress slowed to a virtual crawl for an embarrassingly long time. In fact, decades. Eventually, I rediscovered training less frequently and started making some of my best progress ever. Well into middle-age, when the pundits would have you believe progress has to slow or even stop, I'm getting bigger and stronger and more muscular than at any other time in my life, which is exciting—and more than a little depressing at the same time.

Muscle soreness has a long history of being used as an indicator of recovery. Unfortunately, it's a useless one. Let me qualify that. If you are sore from a workout, it is guaranteed you have not recovered from the workout. Conversely, however, being "not sore" is no indicator that you have recovered. As a matter of fact, you can prevent—or greatly reduce—soreness simply by training frequently. Arthur Jones would often remark on this fact.

When he resumed training again after a long layoff, he would train every day for the first week to prevent debilitating soreness. He knew those workouts were not as productive as they might have been due to being too frequent, but he also knew that excessive muscle soreness would impinge on his ability to go all-out in his workouts. So his first week of training was always geared toward ramping up without having to cope with extreme soreness.

This phenomenon has been recognized for decades, and I even wrote about it twenty years ago in articles I penned for major bodybuilding magazines. In the old days they used to call it a "feeder" workout: you'd train really hard, and then come back later in the day, 4 to 6 hours later, and train the same body parts again but at a lower intensity. The theory was that the later workout pumped fresh blood and nutrients into the stressed muscles, "feeding" them. This system stopped muscle soreness pretty much in its tracks so we all thought it was enhancing recovery. I wish I had back some of the hours I wasted.

> EVENTUALLY, I REDISCOVERED TRAINING LESS FREQUENTLY AND STARTED MAKING SOME OF MY BEST PROGRESS EVER.

> I WISH I HAD BACK SOME OF THE HOURS I WASTED.

There is a method for monitoring the state of your recovery that I experimented with and wrote about years ago: it should indicate when you've fully recovered from a workout. The theory is that your resting heart rate will be influenced by the level of physical trauma throughout your overall system. The only issue is that you need a uniform method of taking heart rate. By that I mean that if you check it during the day, it will change depending

> MUSCULAR GROWTH AND STRENGTH REQUIRE PROPER RECOVERY; *ERGO* IF YOU ARE NOT STRONGER, YOU'VE PROBABLY NOT RECOVERED.

on how the rest of your day is going. The only reliable benchmark is to take your pulse first thing when you wake up in the morning. Pulse rate surges a bit when you first wake up, so first thing means to lie in bed for a minute or two after waking up and then take your pulse.

The other requirement, obviously, is that you can't be overtraining when you start this or it will skew the results. You'll need to take a week off from training, at least. If you even suspect you might be overtraining, better make it two. Then take your pulse every morning for a solid week. Take the average. Going forward, any time your pulse is elevated by more than a few beats per minute, you know you're in an overtrained state. Your next workout comes the day that you wake up with your pulse back to normal. I always felt pretty confident that this worked, but I confess that it didn't take long before I felt it was just too much of a hassle and I stopped.

There is one sure indicator (after the fact) of full recovery. It is pretty simple, really. Muscular growth and strength require proper recovery; *ergo* if you are not stronger, you've probably not recovered. Just look at the frequency that you currently work out. If you go more than a couple workouts without making noticeable improvement in strength levels, you are probably working out too frequently. Or, you are dogging it during your workouts. But in all likelihood, if you are serious enough to be reading this magazine in the first place, taking it easy in your workouts probably isn't your thing. If you are failing to make the progress you used to, try shortening the duration of your workout and reducing frequency, and see what happens. M

*Note: The Arthur Jones reference was drawn from arthurjonesexercise.com assembled by Brian D. Johnston.

Foundations:
The Kettlemill Challenge

Jon Bruney

I would like to share with you a very demanding conditioning workout called the kettlemill challenge. This routine will produce results quickly. If you push yourself on this workout, you will see fat loss, accelerated recovery, and an improved mental outlook.

To take on the kettlemill challenge, you will need two kettlebells (of the same weight), a treadmill, and a timer; a heavy bag is optional. A treadmill is essential because it will force your body to maintain a certain speed. The kettlemill challenge is a hybrid conditioning routine combining timed rounds of kettlebell exercises and running intervals on the treadmill. To get the most out of this program, there should be no breaks in between rounds.

To begin, perform double kettlebell snatches. Swing the kettlebells between the legs and explosively drive the bells over your head. Lower the bells to the shoulders and repeat. Your goal is to perform as many double snatches as possible in 3 minutes. If you need help with technique, pick up one of Pavel Tsatsouline's excellent kettlebell training books or MILO articles.

Next, get on the treadmill for 5 minutes at a minimum pace of 5 mph. Your goal on the treadmill is to run as fast as possible for the entire 5-minute interval.

Once you get off the treadmill, pick up your kettlebells and clean them to the rack position. Lower the bells and repeat. Perform the double cleans for as many reps as possible in 3 minutes.

Immediately following the double-clean interval, get back on the treadmill. Run at your maximum pace for another 5 minutes.

Next, perform the double kettlebell squat and push press combo. Take two kettlebells and clean them to the rack position. Perform a front squat. When you come out of the squat, explosively press the bells overhead in lockout position. Do as many repetitions as possible in 3 minutes.

Now do another 5-minute interval on the treadmill. By now your cardiovascular system will be in overdrive. After the treadmill interval, perform double kettlebell swings. Pick up the kettlebells and swing them between your legs, making sure to drive the kettlebells with your hips. Perform as many repetitions as possible in 3 minutes.

Next, perform the final 5-minute treadmill interval.

Now comes the optional bonus round. Perform heavy bag punch-and-kick combinations for 2 to 3 minutes. You will feel the power of the kettlemill challenge the first time you try it.

To increase the difficulty of the kettlemill challenge, you can do the following: increase the kettlebell weight, increase the treadmill speed, or increase the treadmill incline. Make sure you put the kettlemill challenge into your strength and conditioning arsenal.

The kettlemill challenge:

- double KB snatches – as many as possible in 3 min.
- 5-min. treadmill interval
- double KB cleans – as many as possible in 3 min.
- 5-min. treadmill interval
- double KB squat and push press combo – as many reps as possible for 3 min.
- 5-min. treadmill interval
- double KB swings – as many as possible in 3 min.
- 5-min. treadmill interval
- optional: 2 to 3 min. heavy bag interval

Note: There are no breaks in between rounds.

Enjoy the challenge! M

Why Systematic Development of Trainees is the Superior Methodology

Steven Helmicki

Author of *The Art of the Neck: Training for Distortion* and *Primordial Strength System*

"Against the tide we swim with tools that make us sink."

The performance market has become driven by tools created first—with subsequent methodologies as an accessory. It is inverse to the way effective training should be constructed. First come the superior methodologies. These lead to the development of carefully constructed tools that are integral to achieving high performance—not that are attachments to average mechanical-engineering devices that offer no substantive athletic performance markers except as a contest for max efforts. The slow-twitch trainees and average Daves keep pitching that there is no holy grail, happy to maintain the status quo. But the industry as a whole should be working to create a model that takes into account all relevant factors that go into systematically developing superior athletic talent.

It is too socialist of an idea for some, but the sporadic hodgepodge of trends we have in the U.S. today is ridiculous. High levels of integration of all the relevant developmental factors in strength training will only increase its effectiveness. To believe that everything has already been done in the advancement of training is to believe that the present state of training in the U.S. is as good as it gets. Incoming and new beliefs are never evaluated and overturned by facts. The most patriotic act this industry can make is to provide superior training that is the global standard for our youth and citizens.

"The ability to fully and effectively utilize one's motor potential for achieving success is the essence of sport-technical mastery. This ability is realized by means of a concrete system of movements and appropriate criteria, the composition and organization of which are determined by the type of athletic activity." (Verkhoshansky, *Fundamentals of Special Strength-Training in Sport*)

The training conclusion

Despite the fact that numbers in the 225-lb. bench press for reps and 40-yard dash times are all the rage, training for those numbers correlates little to actual sports performance. They are distinct types of performances. The average pass in the NFL is estimated at 6.5 yards. The key is for the receiver to separate from the pack and the defensive back to close in on the receiver—again and again with dominance—in this range. Drill this repeatedly in training instead of conducting tests. The popularity of these misguided measures has set up a cottage industry of people who specifically train for testing performance rather than field performance. Within that realm, the testing forms are constantly manipulated in order to amplify the effectiveness of various guru tricks.

Instead, set up training that drills repeated outputs in quick fashion, since plays begin and end quickly, a cycle that is repeated over and over again.

Better tests would be:

- 6 random distance sprints relative to the sport for a combined time with rest periods akin to the sport
- a Landmine press for measured speed and power 10 times with 5 seconds of rest in between attempts
- shot put throws overhand and backhand 6 times in a row for combined measurement
- 10 continuous broad jumps, and 10 repeated vertical jumps

Again, the search is for repeatability measures that are not excessively hard on the body but difficult enough to be relevant to demonstrating explosive power–endurance adequately. Field-related markers are the key to establishing the relevancy of training. Some of the factors to consider when devising training and testing are:

1. risk to reward
2. portability/transferability of skill improvement
3. place in an athletic career
4. compression of athletic mortality
5. continuous super-compensation of type II B fibers
6. improved communication and trust between performance coaches and sport-specific coaches through discernable transferability of training
7. improved communication and trust between athlete and strength coach through discernable transferability of training
8. maintenance of an athlete's concentration through variability
9. chronic evolving quickness
10. absorption and dissipation of contact, and
11. time constraints

Those who thrive on evaluating non-time sensitive absolute maximums and slow-twitch endurance markers should go play short space basketball and establish the connectivity of what they are doing. Play consistently with athletes who train for explosive power–endurance and see how you compare. You may end up saying the irrelevant, "Although you beat me, I can still do 225 lb. for more reps than you."

Defining explosive power–endurance

"The prolonged ability to produce explosive power output in athletics developed through speed–strength and strength–speed maximization is achieved through small and large complex training based in shock and variable advancement with minimum rest periods in phases that consistently irritate the organism to maximize super compensation over the lifetime of the athlete." (from the Primordial Strength System Intermediate Certification presentation)

Athletic planning

It is not a new trend—it is a necessity, and no better assessment tool exists than the SWOT analysis. This tool should be started at the bridge of youth and basic training, not at a latent state, but not so early as to evoke pressure and anxiety that will become performance inhibitors. The strengths, weaknesses, opportunities, and threats to any athlete should be consistently evaluated.

"Coach–goal–athlete synergy is absolutely necessary, and confidence in the approach will ease the athlete into the trust mindset because the training approach is all-encompassing chronic growth." (from the Primordial Strength Systems Intermediate Certification presentation)

Emotional state

"The force displayed by a man is to a significant degree determined by his emotional state. Strong positive emotions can instantaneously increase the energy of muscular contractions four times." (M. I. Vinogradov, 1966)

The use of the emotional freedom technique has had an astounding impact on me after years of severe performance anxiety in athletic competition. It is used at the youth development stage to invoke ongoing positive states and remains an established part of sports performance training on a daily basis. This, coupled with the use of sports psychologists and readings such as *Winning Ways: How to Succeed in the Gym and Out*, by Randall J. Strossen, Ph.D., creates the opportunity not only for the best emotional states in sports but also for every aspect of life.

Hydration and restoration

Consistent forced hydration breaks are the most effective behavioral modification technique that carries over to the sports season because it is part of the training construct and becomes habitual. During the later period of each training session, restorative nutrients are introduced and immediately followed by stretching, massage, ice baths, contrast therapy, rolling out of trigger points with the stick, etc. Athletes are taught personal responsibility for restoration measures that can be individually managed by allotting specific planned time for them in every workout. Simple and progressive nutritional interventions that can be indoctrinated over time have a greater likelihood of becoming integral to the athlete's lifestyle.

We must stop labeling ourselves as thinkers if we do not believe in the possibility of an ever-changing and superior system that manages the whole development of an athlete. It has been used with great success in Europe and possibilities of greater models remain for those who are committed to creativity and critical thinking. If you do not remain open and analyze beneath appearances, you have become part of a dismissive status quo that will help erode that which you say you love: strength training. Train to win. Period. *Polski energii.*

Spotlight on Strength and Skill

Dr. Ken E. Leistner
Chiropractor

The statements I've made in the past few issues of MILO have raised the hackles of some strength and conditioning coaches. Allow me, please, to first state that yes, MILO is standard reading material for professionals in the field—unlike, for example, *Men's Hairstyling, Fitness,* and *What to Wear* magazines. Believe it or not, the men and women responsible for the strength, conditioning, and health of collegiate and professional athletes don't read "that stuff," and MILO is referred to as a standard.

That some have taken me to task as being overly critical of the direction that the profession has wandered off in during the past decade has made for spirited exchanges, so some history is in order—to give a more meaningful perspective, especially to those who train but don't coach. The strength and conditioning professional has a thankless task, one that is underappreciated by the players they work with and the coaches they serve. Everyone is an expert, providing opinions and input in meetings, but it is the strength and conditioning coach who has to plan, direct, coordinate, and complete the training programs of up to 120 players, for example. Even with the assistance of a staff, this is an accomplishment that is astonishing if done correctly and safely, and those on the outside truly don't understand it. For these reasons, strength and conditioning coaches have my respect. Here is some background information for our readers.

There were numerous individuals who served as "consultants" or *de facto* strength advisors to some college and professional football teams, but Alvin Roy, a consultant and part-time coach himself, is generally recognized as the profession's first strength coach. Boyd Epley, on September 15, 1969, became the first officially hired and paid full-time strength coach at the collegiate level while working with athletes at the University of Nebraska.

Others who helped the many football coaches and programs at all levels across the country in the late 1950s through the 1960s were sought out because they were seen by the football coaches as the only "legitimate lifting guys," thus leaving the field, by default, almost exclusively to those with an Olympic-style weightlifting background. Powerlifting was not yet an established sport, and bodybuilding was viewed in a manner that was

---

. . . BUT IT IS THE STRENGTH AND CONDITIONING COACH WHO HAS TO PLAN, DIRECT, COORDINATE, AND COMPLETE THE TRAINING PROGRAMS OF UP TO 120 ATHLETES, E.G., FOOTBALL PLAYERS.

to be expected by football coaches, so one would not look for advice to come from that branch of the Iron Game tree.

The above synopsis explains why Olympic-style lifts formed the basis of strength training for football when the movement toward having some type of strength program evolved. As power-lifting became entrenched and popular, many devotees became involved with strength coaching, and the bench press especially became a popular and often utilized lift for football players. Thus, from its genesis in the late 1960s, when the strength and conditioning program became part of training for football, through the end of the 1990s, the lifting part—the strength aspect—of strength and conditioning was the emphasized part of the players' preparation.

Traditionally, the football coaches handled the conditioning end of the equation. The actual football coach, the head coach and his position coaches, were always the ones who designed various distance running (a popular approach for a number of decades to prepare for a short-sprint based activity) and sprints, specific conditioning drills, running-based technique, and "toughening-up" and punishment drills that were included in an effort to get the team and individual players ready to participate in football practice and games. It wasn't until the 1980s that the conditioning aspect of strength and conditioning actually fell under the responsibility and supervision of the strength and conditioning coaching staff.

Unfortunately, if the strength aspect had been overly stressed for the first few decades of the profession, the de-emphasis of the strength end of things—and what I believe to be an over-emphasis on the conditioning aspect—eventually took root and eroded the most valuable and most malleable part of a player's preparation. Much of the time put into strength improvement is technique work done in an attempt to enhance existing levels of strength. However, this is work on movements that actually prevent the athlete from working to his or her maximal ability or intensity, and that is why one can state that strength training has gone soft. Much of the time put into the entire physical preparation period for the majority of athletes is spent in the weight room performing exercises with balls, bands, and a variety of doo-dads that guarantee submaximal effort instead of training to become stronger—and that is why one can state that strength training has gone soft. Much of the strength and conditioning time period is spent out of the weight room, and again that is why one can state that strength training has gone soft.

> When much of the strength and conditioning time, period, is spent out of the weight room, one can state that strength training has gone soft.

There are a few superb strength and conditioning coaches who can de-emphasize the strength aspect of the program and win. The University of Southern California's terrific Chris Carlisle is one—in part because he is smart and insightful and in part because the team gets excellent physical material to work with. Understand that there are strength coaches who get material every bit as physically talented as USC with the potential to be as

The great strength and conditioning facility of Michigan State University.

Michigan State linebacker Greg Jones building the "physical plant" specifically for football.

Offensive tackle John Deyo benching as part of his off-season training at Michigan State University.

Head strength and conditioning coach Ken Mannie pushes his Michigan State Spartans to the limit.

Michigan State Spartan Andre Anderson under the squat bar.
Photos courtesy of Ken Mannie.

The wonderful history and tradition of college football can offer a lifetime of learning and enjoyment for those who pursue it. There are groundbreakers on the field and in the background, and for those who are not involved in this specialized pursuit, Ken Mannie's name may not mean a lot. To those who know, however, Coach Mannie is a thinker, motivator, educator, and superior communicator. A native of the great football hotbed of Steubenville, Ohio, Coach Mannie utilized weight training to go from a walk-on to a three-year starter as an offensive lineman at the University of Akron. He began as a successful high school teacher and coach, and after graduate work and going through the coaching ranks at Akron, Ohio State, and Toledo under Nick Saban, he landed at Michigan State where he has directed the strength and conditioning program for the past fifteen years. A prolific author and lecturer, his belief in hard, intense work, and scientifically supported methods has produced a plethora of professional players.

muscularly large and strong and fast—they just don't do the job as effectively as Coach Carlisle does. There are those who cannot recruit the type of athletes who attend and play for USC, with Stanford being the obvious example in the same conference. Academic standards that place Stanford in the top five nationally for admissions just don't allow for the number of physically gifted players that a USC, UCLA, or Oregon will have in any season.

These programs cannot do things exactly as USC does, but Coach Carlisle can and does spend most of his time on what could be termed movement skills and movement improvement. He can, in fact, get his athletes strong enough to play against anyone, and focus on getting them faster, quicker, and more agile, and develop what I will call a better sense of their bodies and kinesthetic movement patterns. However, most programs are not USC, most coaches are not Chris Carlisle. Most programs that have abandoned a true commitment to make their players as strong as possible for an emphasis on other physical qualities could improve what is being done.

The exercises chosen, the modalities used, and the actual sets and reps vary in almost every strength and conditioning program in the nation. Because each coach of a professional team or major university program puts his or her own twist on things (often for baffling reasons other than the possible distinction of telling others "we do it my way"), there is no one typical collegiate football strength training program. If one were to attend a coaches' convention and corner six leaders of the most prestigious programs in the country, and all shared the same basic training and exercise selection philosophy, the programs may still bear little resemblance to each other. The uninitiated (meaning anyone with a long history and interest related to lifting weights, but who has not participated as a player, coach, or consultant to one of these programs) may also fail to realize that each program differs phase to phase, season to season, and position by position, and then takes into consideration both injury trends related to that specific position and physical limitations of individual players. Did I mention that the personal likes and dislikes of the head coach, a coordinator, or position coach will also dictate aspects of the program?

Sample workout

The following sample workout is taken from the highly successful program of a university that competes in one of the elite bowl championships series conferences and was performed as part of the summer pre-season program.

Exercise	Sets x Reps
Neck flexion	1 x 8–12
Neck extension	1 x 8–12
Neck right lateral flexion	1 x 8–12
Neck left lateral flexion	1 x 8–12
Shrug (modality of choice)	1 x 8–12
Deadlift	1 x 8–10; 1 x 6–8; 1 x 4–6 (3 sets total)
Leg curl	1 x 8–10
Leg extension	1 x 10–12
Dumbbell lunge	1 x 10; 1 x 8; 1 x 6
Leg press	2 x 10–12
Abdominal crunch	1 x 100

Of course, more is coming in the next issue of MILO.

My Dinnie Quest, or Two Years Within
The Brotherhood of Stone

Roger Davis

It is not often in life that you can remember the exact point in time that you start on a far-reaching and life-changing journey, but in my case, I can remember the moment that I began a two-year training quest to lift the Dinnie Stones. It also marked the beginning of my comradeship with The Brotherhood of Stone.

It was a telephone call that did it. I had just returned from Scotland following my successful lift of the Inver Stone ["A Stone Lifter's Holiday," MILO, March 2008, Vol. 15, No. 4], when I gave my friend Steve Angell a ring to let him know about the trip.

"That's great," said Steve, "well done. But did you manage to get up to Potarch?"

"No, we didn't get that far," I said, "We had a long drive back from Inver."

"Oh, that's a shame," said Steve, and here comes the phrase that was to shape my life for the next two years. "In my opinion, lifting the Inver Stone is very rewarding, but if you can lift the Dinnie Stones without straps and a belt, also being 100% drug-free, that is the pinnacle of stone lifting in my book, and deserving of entry into The Brotherhood of Stone."

Steve is a man whom I admire a lot. He does not give praise easily and values actions above words, as his own achievements in all-round lifting have shown ["Steve Angell, All-Round Champion," MILO, June 2001, Vol. 9, No. 1]—and if he declared the lifting of the Dinnie stones as a worthy target, then I wanted to achieve it.

Dinnie Stones: two massive stones with large rings attached

smaller   321 lb. (146 kg)
larger   413 lb. (187.5 kg)

So there I was. The scars had not yet healed from my encounter with the Inver Stone, and I already had a new goal. Life is good when you know where you want to go.

My first Dinnie-focused training session began on 15 August 2007, just three days after my encounter with the Inver Stone. I had already decided that to lift the Dinnie Stones, two things were required: one, a world-class grip, and two, a back capable of performing very heavy deadlifts or partial deadlifts.

In my opinion, if you can close the No. 3 Captains of Crush Gripper with each hand and lift over 300 kg on the deadlift, I would say that you had a good shot at lifting the Dinnie Stones without any specific training. As I had a starting point of 10 reps with the No. 1 CoC gripper and a beltless deadlift of around 200 kg, I realised that I would have to put in some serious specific training.

My first month of training included grip-based work on the Rolling Thunder® revolving deadlift handle and the decision to work all deadlifts using the front knuckle grip to help improve my hand strength at the same time as working my back. My Rolling Thunder work was 55 kg for 10 reps each hand; my front knuckle deadlift a mediocre 170 kg; and my first attempt with the IronMind R-Ring to duplicate the Dinnie Stone lift was a pitiful 125 kg. My journal read, "Very hard lift with ring; must get to 155 kg."

It was in this first month that I began to realise the magnitude of what I was trying to achieve and how far short I currently was. My thoughts got a bit despondent, and I began to lose confidence in my abilities.

At this point I turned to some of my stone lifting brothers on John Brookfield's stone lifting forum [www.powerropes.com]. I had already made some good friends in like-minded (or crazy-minded) people on this forum during my training to lift the Inver Stone, and just to set the tone as to what type of people they are, here are a few comments:

"Stone lifting is more than just lifting heavy stones, it's about overcoming obstacles, it's about finding strength in yourself, it's about pushing your own limits . . . and it's about history. The stones you lift may have never been lifted before or maybe they have . . .

but by whom? And why? The stone lifters of the past speak to us through this conquest, as we have termed them 'The Brotherhood of Stone.'"
—Erik Suave (USA)

"Lifting stones is about far more than just the physical challenge of the 'LIFT.' For me it embraces a history that weaves its way back through thousands of years, to a time when man had little else to prove his strength and manhood other than the ability to lift the heaviest stone the Earth could provide him. Once you have lifted natural stone there is no going back . . . for anyone who is struggling to find what is given for free by nature to lift . . . keep on searching, it's worth the weight [sic]."
—Regan Bridge (New Zealand)

"This is The Brotherhood of Stone at its finest. From across great distances, bonds are formed. A man overcomes obstacles, travels to another continent, and faces a supreme challenge. Then he has the courage to tell others how he did and on top of that, he thanks them for their inspiration. Character of this sort is rare in our world today. But thankfully The Brotherhood of Stone has such men."
—Bill Crawford (USA)

It was to this group of people that I confided that I was having doubts in my abilities. "After all," I said, "most of the people who had lifted the Dinnie Stones were 20-stone Highland Games athletes or competitive strongmen. I am just a 12-stone auditor who dabbles in all-round weightlifting."

The response was just what I needed to give me a kick up the pants, and it was the straight-talking Steve Angell who gave it to me. "Roger, as I said to you before your trip to the Inver Stone, to lift it you have to believe you can do it. It seems you are already looking for excuses not to lift the Dinnie Stones. Going on about how little you weigh is a poor excuse. Jack Shanks lifted them at a lighter bodyweight than you, and if you look on the Dinnie website, there are others who have lifted them at or around your bodyweight. There are no big men or little men in the world; there are winners and losers. Be a winner, Roger."

This was just what I needed, and the next three months saw an improvement in attitude and in lifting. I pushed my Rolling Thunder work up to 70 kg x 10 reps each hand, my front knuckle deadlift up to 175 kg for 10 singles, and the Dinnie ring work up to 130 kg and 140 kg left and right hand respectively.

It was at the end of 2007 that I became very inspired by Matt Waldron (Australia) on the stone lifting forum. He is a similar-sized lifter to me, had set himself the challenge of lifting the Dinnies the year before, and was approaching the end of his year-long training regimen to prepare himself for his Christmas visit to Scotland. We exchanged numerous training experiences, including how, when training with Dinnie rings, you should keep one weight 30% heavier than the other to simulate the Dinnie stone weight differentials; and details like which brand of hand cream to use to keep your hands soft so that they do not continually tear open under the continued Dinnie ring tribulation.

It was fantastic then, when Matt managed to lift the Dinnie Stones four times with no belt and no straps. Matt really led the way and paved the road of possibility for me. Another lifter who inspired me at this time, and one who was to pick up the torch of the stone lifting brotherhood and spread the word with a zealous fervour, was Bill Crawford, who also managed to lift the Dinnie Stones unassisted in the same month.

The start of 2008 was very positive—not only had I been inspired by the achievements of my stone lifting brothers, but an unlooked-for gift from one of the greatest naturally strong and generous-natured individuals I know was to drive me on even further. After a brief communication by e-mail and my explanation of my Dinnie goal, a set of Dinnie stone replica rings and pins was delivered to my door from Laine Snook, a true gesture of encouragement from a stone lifting brother, and one that was to help me progress further.

The following six months saw some real gains. I purchased a plate-loading grip machine, which really made an impact on my grip strength, and I also incorporated the partial straddle lift—one of the most helpful to the Dinnie Stone lifting position—into my training regimen. It grew from 240 kg to 280 kg during this period. On the rings (which I was training 2 to 3 times per week) I managed a 150-kg lift with the left hand, a 160-kg lift with the right, and a combined lift of 290 kg, which I calculated as being some 87% of the Dinnie Stone weight. The target was getting closer.

My Dinnie-based training was interrupted for a number of weeks in May 2008 with my participation in the Viking Stone Lifting Challenge in Iceland, as promoted and reported by Bill Crawford ["The Viking Stone Lifting Challenge: A New Icelandic Saga," *MILO*, September 2008, Vol. 16, No. 2]. This was, and still remains, one of the most memorable events in my life—both for the sights and experiences of Iceland as well as the lifelong friendships made.

Unfortunately, it made a real dent in my Dinnie progress and despite going back to where I had left off, I found that I could just not get back to the level I was at before the trip.

The added complications that I was beginning to suffer both physically and mentally from almost a year of such focused training, and that my hands were regularly splitting open in four or five consistent points every time I handled the rings brought on a low point. I needed another boost.

It was around this time that Laine Snook accomplished the tremendous feat of putting the Inver Stone overhead, the fourth man in history to do so. When on the forum he stated that he had used a picture of me lifting the Inver Stone, along with the Steve Jeck poem "Rest While You Can," as inspiration during his training. I was honoured—maybe this brotherhood thing works both ways.

Just to give my body a change, I returned to high-rep stone lifting for a month to increase my cardiovascular endurance and give my hands a rest. On 3 July 2008 I managed to lift my 85-kg granite sphere 301 times onto a wine barrel at my daughter's school fair. It took 3 hours to do so, and I raised £700 sponsorship money for the school and a children's charity at the same time. It's funny how a change is as good as a rest, and I felt re-energised for the next six months.

I decided that I had to make my training even more specific, and therefore solicited the help of my brother-in-law, Chris, to help me drill out my 140-kg Nettleden Ham stone [see "Letters to the Editor," MILO, September 2007, Vol. 15, No. 2]. It took over two hours and two tungsten drill bits until I finally had a hole that I could put a loading

Roger Davis lifting an 85-kg granite stone 301 times for charity.
Ben Chehade photo.

Lifting the drilled-out Nettleden Ham stone for specific Dinnie Stone training. Ben Chehade photo.

pin through to attach my Dinnie rings.

For the next six months I would lift this stone twice per week during my 5-mile early morning walks with my good friend Graham and his dog, Jake. Although not from a lifting background at all, Graham soon got behind the strange spectacle and encouraged me on each lift, and more so as I added sandbags to increase the challenge. I consider Graham an honorary member of The Brotherhood of Stone for his help and support.

This training continued, on and on, relentless, changing only when I added new training equipment to my arsenal, including Eagle Loops™ straps, which I used to strengthen the fingers on straddle lifts of up to 240 kg, and a No. 2 Captains of Crush Gripper, which I managed to take to 11 reps. I still had not reached my high point on the rings before the Iceland trip, but I decided that I really must step up to the challenge and set my date with the Dinnies.

The date was 14 December 2008, and one that will stay in my mind. Over 16 months of training had led to that point and now it was to culminate in this one moment. Laine Snook and another stone lifting brother, Alan Wyne, accompanied me. As I reached down to grasp the smaller stone in front of me and the larger behind, I felt the power of the previous stone lifting warriors surge through me—as Bill Crawford had predicted. I set myself and stood. The smaller stone rose from the ground, but the larger remained planted; it moved, it hovered, but it did not break free. I gave it all I had, resulting in my blacking out and Laine Snook catching me as I fell backward.

I made a further seven attempts (including three more blackouts), but the same thing happened on each occasion—the smaller stone left the ground, but the larger stone remained defiant. I was devastated.

I tried to remain positive as I watched Laine Snook easily lift the stones on his first attempt. Alan also managed to lift

Roger Davis on his first attempt with the Dinnie Stones. Conrad Snook photo.

the stones with straps. Inside, I was crushed. Steve's words came back to me, there were winners and losers, and I was a loser.

It was with a heavy heart that I reported back to my brothers, "Attempted to lift the Dinnies eight times, blacked out four times with the effort. Small stone left the ground high on eight occasions, and big stone went 'dit, dit, dit' as it hovered an inch above the ground on each occasion. Close, but not good enough. I am a broken man today!"

I should have expected the response to be encouraging, and it was. Here are two that helped me out the most.

"The morning after the night before is always a good time to reflect on the events that have taken place. Yesterday's adventure, a defeat in your eyes, was in fact a great success. First and foremost, you were there—not by some random series of events, but due to a conscious decision to test yourself against the most fearsome opponent that you will ever meet . . . yourself!

YOU'RE NOT BROKEN . . . JUST BENT. Knowledge is power; what doesn't kill you makes you stronger—if you check, I think you'll find that you still have a pulse and you don't need to be any stronger. I will be there to see you claim your rightful prize—and I'm proud to be your 'brother.'"
—Laine Snook

"Well done on the Dinnies—yeah, I know you didn't quite do it this time, but what matters is you tried. You met the challenge and attempted, which is a hell of a lot more than most people ever do, in anything in their lives. You should be proud; I will leave you with this thought."—Matt Waldron

Matt then quoted the famous Theodore Roosevelt: "It is not the critic who counts; not the man who points out how the strong man stumbles, or where the doer of deeds could have done them better. The credit belongs to the man who is actually in the arena, whose face is marred by dust and sweat and blood, who strives valiantly; who errs and comes short again and again; because there is not effort without error and shortcomings; but who does actually strive to do the deed; who knows the great enthusiasm, the great devotion, who spends himself in a worthy cause, who at the best knows in the end the triumph of high achievement and who at the worst, if he fails, at least he fails while daring greatly. So that his place shall never be with those cold and timid souls who know neither victory nor defeat."

I have this quote printed out and on my gym wall. I look at it often to gain encouragement and would advise all those who are struggling with their own personal goals to do so also. I also received encouragement from another newfound stone lifting brother from Australia by the name of Lance Keen, who made his own pilgrimage to Potarch and a successful lift early in 2009.

After returning to training after the Christmas break, I found that my grip strength was reduced and I could not manage the same weights that I had previously done on the rings. I posted that I had made the decision to make my next attempt at the Dinnies using straps, as I felt that I just did not have the world-class grip in my right hand to lift the larger stone unassisted. I also stated that I felt a bit disappointed in going back on my original goal.

The response from the brotherhood was again most supportive.

"Not a step back, just a smaller step forward. A step forward is a step in the right direction. My favourite lecturer at University had a saying 'If you can't solve the problem—change the problem.' In this case, if getting your grip up to full strength in the timeframe (you set yourself!) isn't possible, then straps are another way of solving the problem of getting the stones off the ground."—Alan Wyne

"Roger, don't concern yourself with the use of straps. I resorted to straps for one reason only . . . I did not know if I'd ever be there again, and those Dinnies were leaving the ground or my arms were leaving their sockets. Life throws us some curve balls every now and then and you never know what comes next. Grab you some while you can! Try it without the straps, but don't feel bad if you end up using them. There's many a man out there who couldn't do them with an engine hoist, never mind with straps! Bask in the glory of standing tall with the famed Dinnies in your hands. Good luck!"—Erik Sauve

It was decided then: my new target was "just to stand tall," and I approached the next six months with renewed vigour that this was more than achievable. Knowing that over half of the lifters featured on the Dinnie web site had used straps made me realize this was still a more than worthy goal to go after.

I also took the advice of Laine and changed my lifting of the stones so that the smaller stone would now be lifted to the rear and used to lever up the larger of the stones. Within three months of using this approach, I managed to lift the equivalent weight of the Dinnies on my combined rings using straps. It had been done in replica; now I had to do it for real.

Using a new position for the partial straddle, to simulate my new position of lifting the Dinnie stones, I managed to hit a new high-water mark of 300 kg in June 2009. I worked my front squat and front knuckle deadlift hard during this period also and managed to lift 150 kg and 202.5 kg, respectively, on these two lifts.

My next attempt at the Dinnie Stones came on 28 June 2009, and I felt more ready than ever. Laine was there to help me, as he had promised, and I felt confident as he strapped me onto the rings. I set myself and then pulled; the small stone came up easily, but I had been there before. I applied all my strength on the larger stone at the front, and to my delight it came up high from the ground. I stood tall for a few seconds to enjoy the moment and then much to the amusement of those watching, including David Webster, I shouted at the top of my voice, "Never give up!" It was a great moment for me, and all of the relentless days of training were nothing but a distant memory.

Dinnie Stone success—one second of triumph makes up for almost two years of training pain. Never give up!
Photo by a friendly bystander.

I managed to lift them with straps once more, and then attempted a lift with no straps; the smaller stone came clean up, but the larger hovered a few centimetres above the ground. A few witnesses, including David Webster and Laine Snook, said that the stone had left the ground, but I know what a good lift is. If you have to lie on the ground and debate whether you have seen daylight or not, it is not a good lift. That would be disrespectful to those who had completed a good, strong, unassisted lift in the past. I had stood tall and that was enough for me.

So there you have it, my two-year Dinnie quest and time spent among The Brotherhood of Stone, a brotherhood that had proved the very meaning of the word by offering encouragement, inspiration, correction, and support in equal measure, a brotherhood that is open to all individuals who take up the challenge of stone lifting in whatever shape and form it may take.

Ultimately, I hope my story may have proved inspirational to you—if a mediocre weightlifter can manage to conquer the almighty Dinnie Stones, anything is possible for you if you put your mind to it. And never, ever, give up. M

2009 Masters' World Championships:
Scottish Master Athletes Gather in the Highlands
William M. Scruggs, Ph.D.

The capital of the Highlands hosted the 9th Masters' World Championships of Scottish heavy athletics as part of the 2009 Homecoming. The Inverness Highland Games, conducted on behalf of the Highlands Council by Gerry Reynolds and Angus Dick, lavishly entertained 83 athletes over the age of 40 from 10 different countries for three days while the athletes put on a great show of skill and strength for the crowd at Bught Park. Eleven world champions were crowned, and in the process they broke 8 masters' world records. Beginning with the provost Jimmie Gray's welcome dinner on Friday and continuing until the final awards on Sunday evening, the athletes were feted on a scale not seen before nor likely to be seen again.

Of all the 11 champions, only 2 emerged without a single event defeat. Jason Young (Scotland), who celebrated his fortieth birthday on Saturday, was totally dominant in the 40-44 age class, winning all events by wide margins. For the 65-69 age class, Ray Oster (USA) won 7 events outright but was tied with Rob Ritchie (Scotland) in the caber. In the process Oster broke both the 16-lb. open stone and the 22-lb. Braemar stone age-class world records. For his record-breaking efforts, Oster received the Caledonian Club of Sacramento's John Ross–Combined Distance Award.

40–44 class
Behind Young in the age 40-44 group, Warren Trask (Canada) finished a fairly easy second with 21 points. Trask was consistent throughout with 5 seconds and 2 thirds. Third place was a hard fought toss-up for the full two days with Uli Mueller (Germany) emerging the winner at 40.5 points, ahead of Rob Hatch (USA) and Kengo Kubota (Japan), who had 42 and 44 points respectively, for fourth and fifth. Bill Stillwell (USA) was sixth with 49 points.

45–49 class
In the 45-49 age class Mark McDonald (Scotland) captured his third masters' world championships by a narrow margin. Berle Conrad (Canada) and Gene Flynn (USA) took the fight to the last event. The three finished with McDonald in first (3 firsts and 18.5 points), Conrad in second (2 firsts and 20.5 points) and Flynn in third (22.5 points). All three placed in the top four for all 8 events. Steve Whyte (England) played the spoiler in

3 events with 2 firsts and a third to finish in fourth overall with 40 points. Malcolm Cleghorn (Scotland) and Brent Abbott (USA) were fifth and sixth, respectively.

50–54 class

A real battle developed between Al Stagner (USA) and Hans-Dieter Dorow (Germany) in the 50–54 age class. The two went back and forth all weekend with each winning 4 events. But the stones proved to be Dorow's downfall as he fell to fourth place in both. Stagner, with 4 firsts and 4 seconds, garnered the world championships with 12 points, and Dorow settled for second with 16 points. Kevin Youngberg (USA) finished third with 29.5 points, just ahead of Bob Vail (USA) with 31 points. Rick Kramer (USA) and Chuck Livingston (USA) rounded out the top six.

55–59 class

This class was dominated by three former world champions, and the closeness of the competition reflected just that. Starting with the caber, Frank Henry stumbled and finished seventh. This hole proved too deep to dig out of for the two-time masters' world champion. But try hard he did, winning 3 events and 2 seconds. Meanwhile, Mark Buchanan, who won here in 2006, won the caber and was off to a great start. Buchanan finished Saturday 1 point ahead of three-time champion Bill Leffler, but Buchanan would win only 1 more event on Sunday. Buchanan picked up 2 seconds and 3 thirds, but Leffler won 3 events, 2 seconds and 3 thirds, to find the needed margin, and he won his fourth world championships (third in class) with 16 points to Buchanan's 19 and Henry's 20. Stan Pike (Scotland), Ron Heaton (England), and Dave Glasgow (USA) filled out the top six.

60–64 class

Wayne Staggs (USA) swept 4 events the first day in this class. But former world champion under 200 lb. Ali Munro (Scotland) spoiled the clean sweep with a win in the light hammer. Meanwhile those two, plus James MacBeath (Scotland), were just inches apart in almost every event to provide an exciting finish between the three. Staggs was the winner with 10 points, and Munro and MacBeath were second and third with 18 and 20 points. Angus Billy Scruggs (USA) was fourth.

65–69 class

Undefeated through all 8 events and holding two new age-class world records, Ray Oster was the obvious world champion in this group. Second place was not so easily determined. Rob Ritchie (Scotland), who tied with Oster in the caber, added 6 seconds and a third to finish second ahead of two-time world champion Dean Ross (USA) and John Thomson (USA). Ross and Thomson divided the other points to finish third and fourth, in that order.

70+ class

Three countries were represented by the three competitors at 70+. Bill Rogers (USA) emerged the winner with 11 points and the proud half of the first father-and-son dual championships, with Kevin Rogers (see below). Ian Miller (England) finished second with 16 points, and Eddie Mulcahy (Ireland) was third with 21 points in a tussle that was much closer than the points would indicate. I have to say, these guys did have a great time throughout the competition.

1. Jason Young, 40–44.

2. Mark McDonald, 45–49.

3. Al Stagner, 50–54.

4. Bill Leffler, 55–59.

5. Wayne Staggs, 60–64.

6. Ray Oster, 65–69.

7. Bill Rogers, 70+.

8. Bobby Brown, 40–49 under 200 lb.
Wendy Brown photo.

9.–10. Kevin Rogers and Jim Spalding tied in the 50+ under 200 lb.

11. Denise Houseman, women's 40–49.

12. Kris Stuteville, women's 50+.

All photos by William M. Scruggs except where noted.

40–49 under 200-lb. class

This class drew 13 competitors from 4 countries, and the only returning champion was Doug Ballard (USA). In a topsy-turvy class, Ballard won 3 events and added 3 seconds, but he struggled in the hammers with a fifth and a sixth, which proved too much to overcome in the tight competition. Neil McKenzie (Scotland) won both hammers with age-class world records, but could do no better than 5 thirds and a fourth in the other events to fall short of the mark. Newcomer to the MWC, Bobby Brown (Canada) won only 2 events but collected 5 seconds and a fourth to finish with 16 points and the world championships. Ballard was second with 20 and McKenzie was third with 21. Robert Henderson (USA) was fourth with 28. Brian Harrold (Scotland) was fifth and John Jan (Canada), who dropped big pounds to get into the class, was sixth.

50+ under 200-lb. class

There were only three competitors in this class, but between them they owned 8 world championships, so this was going to be a hard struggle. Class veteran and two-time world champion Danny Ellis (USA) couldn't outdo the newcomers and finished third. Meanwhile Kevin Rogers (USA) and Jim Spalding (USA) renewed their multi-year struggle for dominance. Each finished with 4 firsts and 4 seconds for a dead-even tie. This marks Spalding's unprecedented sixth world championships and Rogers' second (his title in 2008 was also a tie, but with Doug Ballard).

40–49 women's class

The women's classes boasted their largest number of competitors in MWC history. With 9 in the 40–49 class and 4 in the 50+ class, they bested their former total by 2. The younger class was once again dominated by Denise Houseman (USA), who won her fourth world championships with 11.5 points by winning four events, tying 1 for first and taking seconds in the other 3. MWC newcomer Linda Kimsey (USA) took second with 18.5 points, and Karyn Dallimore (Canada) finished third overall with a strong 22 points. Becky Wissink (USA), Kym Ross Pollard (USA), and Petra Mueller (Germany) rounded out the top six with 35, 41, and 50 points, respectively.

50+ women's class

Kristine Stuteville (USA) managed to break 4 age-class world records—both hammers and both stones—but even with 5 firsts, she only won the championships by 1 point over last year's champion, Ruth Welding (USA), who had 3 firsts. Sue Hallen (USA) finished a close third, just 5 points off the mark. Sue Sanchez (USA) was fourth. Both Hevy Gear's Bill Anderson–Combined Hammer Award and SAAA's a'Ghaidhealtachd–Combined Stone Award went to Stuteville.

Complete results and photos of this year's MWC can be found at www.scottishmasters.org along with other information for masters' athletes. Executive director Bill Scruggs announced in Inverness that the 10th Masters' World Championships, MWC X, will be held on August 14, 2010, at the Colorado Scottish Festival & Rocky Mountain Highland Games in Highlands Ranch, Colorado, a suburb of Denver. Athletes interested in competing and athletic directors interested in hosting are urged to consult the website listed above for full information. M

Enter the
Kettlebell Plus

Pavel

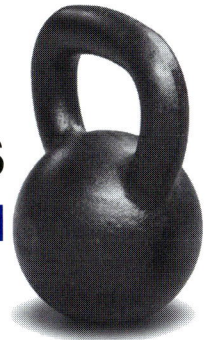

It has been said that Russians create their own problems and then heroically overcome them. The purpose of this article is to solve the non-problem of lack of exercise variety in the *Enter the Kettlebell!* training plan.

The following template addresses dynamic strength, slow strength, and conditioning. It was designed to comply with the training principles known in Russia as "waving the loads," "the continuity of the training process," and "specialized variety." Enjoy the pain!

Since push presses/jerks and squats have been added to pulls and presses, the *Enter the Kettlebell!* schedule needed to be modified to keep the workouts short. Grinds and ballistics have been separated into their own days, each category to be practiced twice a week. To keep complying with the light–medium–heavy effort plan, a micro-cycle has been stretched out to two weeks. On Dan John's recommendation, the order of the sessions has been changed to place the heavy effort in the beginning of the week and the medium effort at the end. This will keep the athlete fresh for a weekend competition. This will also enable him to replace the medium days with light "tonic" workouts when desired.

A pair of dice, as in *Enter the Kettlebell!*, prescribes the duration of an exercise series: 2 to 12 minutes. For simplicity's

Week 1

Monday	Tuesday	Wednesday	Thursday	Friday	Saturday	Sunday
Grinds	Ballistics	Variety	Grinds	Ballistics	Variety	Off
Heavy effort	Light effort		Medium effort	Medium effort		
Press 1 *	Pull		Press 1	Pull		
Squat	Push press/jerk		Squat	Push press/jerk		
Press 2 *			Press 2			
(Pull-up)			(Pull-up)			

Week 2

Monday	Tuesday	Wednesday	Thursday	Friday	Saturday	Sunday
Grinds	Ballistics	Variety	Grinds	Ballistics	Variety	Off
Light effort	Heavy effort		Medium effort	Medium effort		
Press 1	Pull		Press 1	Pull		
Squat	Push press/jerk		Squat	Push press/jerk		
Press 2			Press 2			
(Pull-up)			(Pull-up)			

*Presses are trained twice in one day, an old Russian weightlifting practice. It allows one to be relatively fresh and to practice two different press variations.

sake we will do this for all exercises—the grinds, as well as the ballistics. On the heavy day the trainee is required to do as many reps as possible with the given weight in the specified time frame, as in Charles Staley's Escalating Density Training (EDT). However, he must stick to the ladder protocol, repeating several ladders best suited to get the most reps in the given exercise with the given weight.

For grinds you may not exceed 5 reps per set, even with light bells. Your ladder choices are:

1, 2, 3 (6 reps)
1, 2, 3, 4 (10 reps)
1, 2, 3, 4, 5 (15 reps)

Double kettlebell drills.
Photos courtesy of www.DragonDoor.com.

Restricting the athlete to such ladders will reduce guesswork—"What is the best way to pace myself to get the most reps in 10 minutes?"—and will encourage better technique and higher muscular tension. You do not have to pick the tallest ladder you can do, but the one that allows you to bang out the most reps in the given time frame. It may take some experimentation.

Double kettlebell quick lifts also follow specific ladders, doubling the grinds' reps:

2, 4, 6 (12 reps)
2, 4, 6, 8 (20 reps)
2, 4, 6, 8, 10 (30 reps)

Single kettlebell quick lifts have higher ladders of their own:

5, 10 (15 reps)
10, 15, 20 (45 reps)
10, 20 (30 reps)

Such moderate reps are meant to discourage pacing and to encourage consistently high power output. Don't climb higher on the ladder if your explosiveness drops off. Feel free to shorten the ladders towards the end of the exercise round.

Comments Dan John, Russian Kettlebell Challenge (RKC) Team Leader: "One of the great insights, among many, that I picked up at the RKC is the idea of doing 20 swings with one kettlebell and 10 swings with two kettlebells. After doing literally hundreds of swings a day, I noted that my technique held up fine in that 10 and 20 range. It is the basic teaching of sports: don't let quantity influence quality. In other words, 10 good reps are far better than dozens of crappy reps. If you want more volume, just do more sets.

"Others have noted the same issue. If I can do 100 snatches with the 24 or 16, what additional good will come from doing 120? Yes, I know in competition this is the key, but to the non-GS [*girevoy* sport] athlete, 100 snatches are probably way above the ceiling necessary for improvement. If I can get what I need in 20 snappy swings, why add more reps at the expense of technique?

"Absolutely, there are times when you should do more than 20. There are times when you want to do all kinds of things. There are times, though, known as 'most of the time' where you just keep moving ahead. I usually call these the 'punch the clock' workouts and I think it is the key to staying in the game."

On the heavy-effort day, the trainee is instructed to do as many reps as possible in the given time frame (1 to 12 minutes as determined by a roll of a pair of dice), using prescribed ladders. This is considered a 100% effort. On a medium-effort day the trainee will do 70–80% of the reps he thinks he is capable of, and on the light-effort day he will do 50–60%. "The one thing that people may have a problem with is how to pace themselves for heavy-, medium-, and light-effort days," comments Shaun Cairns, Senior RKC instructor from South Africa. "The way I paced myself is on heavy days (in my rest between ladders) was to walk a short distance and back to the bell, on medium days to walk twice the distance as that of the heavy days, and on light days to walk three times the distance. The initial distance is dependent on your fitness and as you get fitter this distance can be reduced. This ensures that your pace throughout the duration of the exercise is relatively consistent."

The weight of the kettlebells is also prescribed by the dice, this time by a single die. Depending on the number of kettlebells the *girevik* (kettlebell lifter) owns and his ability in the given exercise, he will personally assign the values to each die roll. Be biased toward medium-sized weights.

For example, if the *girevik* owns pairs of 16s, 24s, and 32s and can press a pair of 32s 2 to 3 times, he might assign the following values to various rolls of a die:

1 dot   16s
2 dot   16s
3 dots   24s
4 dots   24s
5 dots   24s
6 dots   32s

Note the emphasis on the 24s.

Double presses, swings, and front squats allow one to use different-sized bells for a unique training effect for the stabilizing musculature. You could try something like this:

1 dot   16s
2 dots   16 + 24
3 dots   16 + 32
4 dots   24s
5 dots   24 + 32
6 dots   32s

If you have chosen two bells of different sizes, switch arms every set. For example, 24 L + 32 R x 1, 24 R + 32 L x 2, 24 L + 32 R x 3; 24 R + 32 L x 1, etc.

When it comes to the double snatch, our comrade can barely snatch a pair of 32s, and only on a good day. This means this weight should be left to variety days. His double snatch assignments would look like this:

1 dot   16s
2 dots   16s
3 dots   16s or 24s
4 dots   24s
5 dots   24s
6 dots   24s

> IF I CAN GET WHAT I NEED IN 20 SNAPPY SWINGS, WHY ADD MORE REPS AT THE EXPENSE OF TECHNIQUE?

Again, each individual exercise should have a separate table of weight values for each roll of a single die. If you can do fewer than 3 perfect reps with a given weight, this weight should be saved for the variety days, as explained in *Enter the Kettlebell!*

The exercise selections in each category (pull, press, squat, and push press/jerk) are also picked with a roll of a single die. This gives you 6 variations to play with, around the sweet spot Mark Reifkind has discovered in his version of Westside training. If there are too many variations (say, 12), you will not be practicing each individual one often enough. With 6 you will. Note that some powerful exercise variations have not made it to the list because they are not similar enough to the basic drill or because they don't allow a high volume. The bottom-up press is a good example. Save such drills for a limited practice on the variety days.

Here are your recommended exercise variations. An experienced trainee may choose to replace some of these with barbell lifts.

Pulls
1 dot	swing, one hand, two hands, or hand-to-hand
2 dots	over-speed two-hand swing with a partner or a Jump Stretch™ band
3 dots	double swing
4 dots	fast cadence snatch (don't pause at the lockout)
5 dots	slow cadence snatch (lift and lower explosively but pause at the lockout for a few seconds)
6 dots	double snatch

Presses
1 dot	clean & press (re-clean the kettlebell before each press rep)
2 dots	military press (clean the kettlebell once and do all the prescribed presses)
3 dots	Pat Casey military press (hold on to a sturdy object at chest level with your free arm; this will allow you to put up more weight)
4 dots	double clean and press

Presses (cont.)
5 dots	high stop alternating military press (lower one kettlebell to your chest and press it back up while holding the other kettlebell overhead)
6 dots	see-saw press ("teeter-totter" the kettlebells, pressing one while simultaneously lowering the other)

Jerks/push presses
1 dot	Viking push press (drop the kettlebell from lockout to your chest, dip your knees, and immediately rebound)
2 dots	double Viking push press (light kettlebells only, speed is of the essence)
3 dots	jerk
4 dots	double jerk
5 dots	double clean and jerk
6 dots	double push press from a full front squat

Squats
1 dot	goblet squat (refer to the writings of Dan John)*
2 dots	goblet squat
3 dots	double front squat
4 dots	double front squat
5 dots	pistol (one-legged rock-bottom squat with the free leg straight out in front)
6 dots	pistol (see 5 dots)

*take a narrow stance; hold the weight at chest height; squat deeply and fluidly as if sitting in a chair; push up explosively with thighs and glutes, maintaining your back position and stance

Adding weighted pull-ups is highly recommended:

Pull-ups
1 dot	tactical pull-up (overhand thumbless grip, no kipping, the neck must touch the bar at the top)
2 dots	chin-up
3 dots	parallel grip pull-up
4 dots	pull-up on rings
5 dots	pull-up on a rope
6 dots	L-seat pull-up

If you have questions about this training plan, don't hesitate to ping me on the www.DragonDoor.com forum.

I have made some of my best gains following a version of this template and I wish you the same. Kettlebell power to you! **M**

2009 USAF Unified National Armwrestling Championships:
Arkansas to Italy—Who's Going?

Denise Wattles
Executive Director,
United States Armwrestling

Little Rock, Arkansas has been the location of the USAF Unified National Championships twice before this year's event and each year has been a record-breaker in attendance. With the state of the economy and the possible expense of traveling to the World Championships (in Porto Viro, Italy), tournament directors Michael and Tonya Todd had expected a smaller turnout at the Unifieds than the previous years.

Weigh-ins started on Thursday night for all of the 57 divisions offered over four days of competition. Any ideas we had about a lack of armwrestlers was quickly dispelled with the arrival of some of the top athletes in the United States for the early weigh-ins. This championships has the reputation of having the toughest competition of any event in the U.S., so the top guns show up early to register in order to have several days to rehydrate, eat, and mentally prepare for the opportunity to make their mark in armwrestling history.

At this tournament there are weight classes for every 10 lb., so many of the competitors have dropped weight for a lower class. I still do not understand why they lose weight to make a lighter class—the men aren't any easier to beat. I guess that is why I am doing the brackets and not the armwrestling!

I have been a part of the staff for 11 of the last 12 Unified National Championships, and I can testify that the classes this year are not only larger, but also deeper than any other year. With larger classes, the athlete must have as much endurance as he does strength and technique in order to place in the top three. Most of those in attendance want to place in the top two so they can represent the U.S. at the Worlds. In addition, this event is also a qualifying event for the Arnold Classic Armwrestling Challenge (ACAC). The top three in all the men's open/senior and ladies' divisions automatically have a place at the Arnold.

> I STILL DO NOT UNDERSTAND WHY THEY LOSE WEIGHT TO MAKE A LIGHTER CLASS—THE MEN AREN'T ANY EASIER TO BEAT.

143-lb. (65-kg) division

Two-time right-hand 132-lb. (60-kg) world champion Vazgen Soghoyan entered the 143-lb. (65-kg) division this year to test his skills against larger men, even though he could have made weight for the lighter class. If he won the class it would mean he would also have to enter the heavier class at the World Championships in Italy. At the World Championships there is a huge difference in strength and ability between these two classes. Apparently Vazgen wasn't concerned about this fact—there was no one at 143 lb. who even slowed him down, and his strength overshadowed any weight he may have given up to his opponents—and he took home a national title in the 143-lb. class for the first time. Corey Ruiz placed second, with Jonathan Gooch placing third.

154-lb. (70-kg) division

I think the most significant upset of the weekend was Ethan Fritsche winning both the right- and left-hand 154-lb. (70-kg) divisions. Still a teenager, Ethan proved that age and experience don't necessarily guarantee a national title. Between the two divisions, Ethan had to face over 25 athletes, but he was undaunted. The records and history of the men in Ethan's classes, including Lee Culpepper, Michael Shaloub, and Chris Thomas, would normally influence the outcome of a class, but not today. Ethan not only beat some of the best, he remained undefeated both right- and left-handed. To say he was stoked is putting it lightly. Not only did he win two national titles, he also put his name on the "hit list" of men to beat in future competitions.

> ETHAN NOT ONLY BEAT SOME OF THE BEST, HE REMAINED UNDEFEATED BOTH RIGHT AND LEFT HAND. TO SAY HE WAS STOKED IS PUTTING IT LIGHTLY.

Michael Shaloub and Ethan had some unbelievable battles, and it was expected that Michael had an edge, but apparently no one had told Ethan. Michael took home second place right-handed and fourth place with his left hand. Lee and Chris didn't even make it to the quarter finals. Armwrestling skill must run in the family: Ethan's dad, Don, is one of the best armwrestlers in the U.S. at 220 lb. In fact, this weekend Don won the master's (age 40+) left-hand 220-lb. class, took second in the open/senior left-hand class, and also placed third in the master's right-hand class. If an athlete wants to improve his skills at armwrestling, I would suggest that he practice with the Fritsches.

176-lb. (80-kg) division

By far the toughest classes to win this weekend were at 176 lb., including the master's and open divisions. Filled with talent, it was a crapshoot as to who would win. Jae-T Hamilton, Ron Erdmann, Justin Joyce, and many other armwrestlers went home without an award despite stellar performances at the table. However, this would be a weekend that Ron Klemba will celebrate for many years to come. Ron, at 53 years of age, made history as the first man ever to win four national titles in one event. Ron won titles in both the right and left hand at 176 lb. in the open and master's divisions. Between these four classes there were almost 60 men who, on any given day, could win their class. I have no doubt that if Ron had entered the grandmaster classes (age 50+), he would have won those also. Luke Kindt did manage to pull his way to second place right hand with Ray Hennerichs finishing third. In the master's divisions John Parton,

> SIMON BERRIOCHOA, USING HIS SIGNATURE "DIVE MOVE,"
> OUT-PULLED EVERYONE BUT RAZOR, FINISHING SECOND
> IN THE RIGHT-HAND CLASS.

who has won this event in the past, had to be satisfied with second place in both arms. The World's will be a challenge for Ron, but after his performance at this event I am not sure that the world is ready for him.

Ron Klemba.
Denise Wattles photos.

187-lb. (85-kg) division
This was one competition where no one class had more intensity than another. Sometimes all anyone can remember and talk about are the super heavyweight battles, but not this weekend. Some of the most impressive matches were between Steve "Razor" Rau and the men he faced. Bryan Johnson, who has been the man to beat at the past Unified Championships, did not perform at his usual level. Left-handed, Bryan was able to qualify for World's with second place, but right-handed, Bryan was put out by the fourth round. Razor had beat Bryan in the second round, and then in the fourth round Brian fell to Bart Wood and was out of the class. Scott Ballinger, son of champion armwrestler Bill Ballinger, has been knocking on the doors of more seasoned athletes, and this weekend he stepped in to make a huge impression on everyone. Scott placed third in both classes despite being the underdog. Simon Berriochoa, using his signature "dive move," out-pulled everyone but Razor, finishing second in the right-hand class. Steve "Razor" Rau won both the right- and left-hand classes. It will be interesting to see if Scott can continue to excel in the future, following in his dad's footsteps.

Bryan Johnson (l.) and Scott Ballinger (r.) prepare for battle.

220-lb. (100-kg) division
This was the first time that Eric Brown had traveled to a large tournament. Eric had been pulling in tournaments in the St. Louis area for a few years and winning, but he had never tested his ability in a major event. An unknown to most, Eric shook up the armwrestling world by winning the open right 220-lb. class, beating several national and world champions in the process. These men didn't have a clue about who Eric was until he pinned them to the pad one by one. Dave

Chaffee, Scott Fleming, and Terry Burgin are just a few who will recognize Eric by name at future events. In his first major competition, Eric walked off with his first national title and the respect that comes with it. Left-handed, 2005 world champion Scott Fleming proved why he holds the title and in the process earned the right to represent the U.S. at another WAF World Championships.

I didn't mean to discount the performance of the super heavyweights earlier in this article. These men are always impressive and leave the spectators with a lot to talk about for days. Richard Lupkes, 53 years old, has won the title in the right-hand supers for the last two years, and it was no surprise that he successfully defended the title this year. There were some doubters because Richard was in a very serious car accident in February and sustained a torn pectoral muscle, which required surgery to repair. Also, it was only a year ago that Richard tore his biceps at this event in Salt Lake City. Obviously he has recovered from these injuries. Don "Hollywood" Underwood armwrestled better that he ever has at the Unifieds, winning the left-hand super heavyweight title. Don is always intense and quick on the go and this year it paid off. I expect this win will give him the incentive to keep practicing and lifting weights.

In September 2009, one of the best armwrestling teams the United States has ever had will travel to Porto Viro, Italy to defend the team champion world title they earned last year in Canada. It won't be an easy task but I think it is a definite possibility that 2009 will be another stellar year.

Billings, Montana has been selected for the 2010 USAF Unified National Championships. Billings is the home of the United States Armwrestling Association, which has been promoting armwrestling for 25 years. Because the 2010 WAF World Armwrestling Championships is being hosted by the Oasis Resort and Casino in Mesquite, Nevada, it is expected that more than 500 athletes will travel to Billings to qualify for Team USA. In the armwrestling world, theoretically, the road to Las Vegas goes through Billings, Montana.

2009 USAF Unified National Armwrestling Championship Results
27–28 June 2009, Little Rock, AR

Men's open right
121-lb.	(55-kg)	Joseph Cordova/ Zach Harrison/ Dallas Hennerichs
132-lb.	(60-kg)	Brent Norris/ Craig Goodwin/ Andrew Schang
143-lb.	(65-kg)	Vazgen Soghoyan/ Corey Ruiz/ Jonathan Gooch
154-lb	(70-kg)	Ethan Fritsche/ Michael Shaloub/ Heath McDonald
165-lb.	(75-kg)	Shawn Dempsey/ Jason Trumbower/ Josh Wood
176-lb.	(80-kg)	Ron Klemba/ Luke Kindt/ Ray Hennerichs
187-lb.	(85-kg)	Steve Rau/ Simon Berriochoa/ Scott Ballinger
198-lb.	(90-kg)	Brent Rakers/ Dan Whittle/ Eric Wolfe
220-lb.	(100-kg)	Eric Brown/ Terry Burgin/ Scott Fleming
242-lb.	(110-kg)	Michael Todd/ Jim Bryan/ Robbie Burnett
243+-lb.	(110+-kg)	Richard Lupkes/ Lindley Keating/ Don Underwood

Men's open left
121-lb.	(55-kg)	Joseph Cordova/ Cody Wagner/ Zach Harrison
132-lb.	(60-kg)	Andrew Schang
143-lb.	(65-kg)	Corey Ruiz
154-lb	(70-kg)	Ethan Fritsche/ Corey Ruiz/ Bill Brown
165-lb.	(75-kg)	Luke Kindt/ Jeremy Plaster/ Josh Wood
176-lb.	(80-kg)	Ron Klemba/ Dan Worley/ Bobby Green
187-lb.	(85-kg)	Steve Rau/ Bryan Johnson/ Scott Ballinger
198-lb.	(90-kg)	Dan Whittle/ Brent Rakers/ Tony Villa
220-lb.	(100-kg)	Scott Fleming/ Britt Dunnigan/ Frank Hurst
242-lb.	(110-kg)	Michael Todd/ Don Fritsche/ Jim Bryan
243+-lb.	(110+-kg)	Don Underwood/ Lindley Keating/ Matt Bertrand

M

How to Generate the Greatest Strength at the Lightest Bodyweight

Steve Justa
Author of *Rock Iron Steel: The Book of Strength*

Generating the greatest strength at the lightest bodyweight is or should be the main goal of every lifter—this is when the body is most efficient and your mind is also. Lugging a whole bunch of excess weight around is counterproductive to everybody; it slows you down. Everybody, or at least the biggest percentage of the population, has the idea that to be really strong you have to be really big. That really isn't the case at all. Yes, it does help your strength to be big, but it slows down and hurts everything else. It increases your chances of getting heart disease or diabetes tremendously. It cuts your oxygen intake efficiency in half. It slows down your recovery time in between workouts, not to mention that it does your sex life absolutely no good at all. Yes, it may be intimidating to your fellow man for you to be huge, but the price you pay isn't worth it. I think you understand what I'm getting at.

When you want to learn something important, I believe you should always try to pick up a few pointers from the elite in the field of your choice. And when you talk the greatest strength at the lightest bodyweight, you have to look at Arthur Saxon, for in my mind he has to rank as one of the greatest strong men who ever lived. At a bodyweight of only about 200 lb., Arthur could put a 371-lb. barbell above his head with one arm, and he could walk with "well over a ton" on his shoulders. I will guarantee you there is nobody alive today that could do that at any weight, let alone at 200 lb.—and this was back in the 1890s before there were any kind of supplements or steroids . . . but I guess Arthur liked his beer.

I read a couple of Arthur's books to pick up some pointers, and what Arthur said makes great sense. He said that no matter how big a muscle is, it does you absolutely no good at all if the tendon connections underneath the muscle aren't tough enough to handle heavy iron. He also said that no matter how big you are, if you haven't got the bodily energy to back it up, being big does not help you at all. Arthur basically said to get great strength at a light bodyweight, you must work every different scrap of muscle you can, and work it directly and thoroughly. Arthur said that fat

> YES, IT DOES HELP YOUR STRENGTH TO BE BIG, BUT IT SLOWS DOWN AND HURTS EVERYTHING ELSE.

> . . . TO GET GREAT STRENGTH AT A LIGHT BODYWEIGHT, YOU MUST WORK EVERY DIFFERENT SCRAP OF MUSCLE YOU CAN, AND WORK IT DIRECTLY AND THOROUGHLY.

cannot exist on a well-exercised muscle for long, and since you have over 650 different muscles in the body, it does involve a lot of work. Arthur said he did every different type of lifting he could think of, trying to pull in every different muscle he could think of, and he said his constant practice and very hard work year in and year out were the keys to super strength. He said that from workout to workout you must always try to increase the weight or the number of times you lift the weight you are already using by doing more sets. This toughens you up and increases your bodily energy.

People who watched Arthur train for 2 or 3 hours in a row used to say that the more he practiced in one session, the stronger he got. This is because he had built up his bodily energy and his will power to such a great point that it enabled him not to tire out, but in fact to get stronger at the end of the workout. When you train in this fashion, you're using your willpower as your steroid, always pushing yourself to do more.

For the amateur lifter, Arthur said you must learn to listen to your subconscious mind. When you feel you are rundown and too tired mentally to train, take 2 days off and rest, and then resume practice. Arthur said to do all kinds of lifts: one-arm lifts, two-arm lifts, carrying weight overhead or in

> ... YOU'RE USING YOUR WILLPOWER AS YOUR STEROID, ALWAYS PUSHING YOURSELF TO DO MORE.

> AS I SAID EARLIER, IF YOU WANT TO LEARN SOMETHING, LEARN IT FROM THE BEST.

front or at your thighs, or walking with weight behind your neck. Do supporting lifts, heavy-overload supporting lifts from the ground, bent-over lifts, standing lifts . . . do about every different kind of lifting you can think of. When Arthur trained, he liked to do heavy singles—a lot of them—for 2 to 3 hours, performing a lot of different exercises. As I said earlier, if you want to learn something, learn it from the best. In my mind Saxon was one of the greatest lifters who ever lived, bar none.

What I learned from Arthur I pass on to you, for lost knowledge happens all the time. Follow this philosophy and plan for 5 years, and I'll almost guarantee you that you'll be moving world-record poundage one way or another. What I have written here is probably the best advice anyone in the world could give you in the quest for super strength at a light bodyweight. Don't just read this article once, read it 20 or 30 times and let it soak in. Remember every little thing I have said here and see it in your mind—then you will be ready to go after your goals. Good luck. M

German Men of Might:
Andreas Maier

Gherardo Bonini

Andreas Maier was one of the most loved German lifters, really a pure amateur. In fact after an initial affiliation with a club, in order to closely manage his restaurant business in the railway station of Pasing near Munich, he competed as unattached but still in connection with all the clubs of the town, and thanks to his skill and friendship, became an idol.

Maier was born in Munich in 1875. He was 1.71 m (5' 7") tall and at 96 kg (212 lb.), he built through tenacity a beautiful physique: chest 118 cm (46"); chest inflated 126 cm (50"); neck 47 cm (18"); calf 42.5 cm (17"); upper arm 44.5 cm (17.5"); and forearm 33.5 cm (13"). Affiliated with the Athletenclub Germania of Munich, he gradually advanced in skill and in the opinions of the experts. In 1900, Maier competed in the great national-level competition of Würzburg, getting some prizes and taking part in a Greco-Roman wrestling event. In 1901, he jerked with two hands 139 kg, a remarkable performance. In 1902, he competed in the European championships of The Hague and was runner-

Artist's rendering of Andreas Maier.
Courtesy of Gherardo Bonini.

up, pressing with two hands 116 kg and jerking 140 kg. Finally, the next year, he won the European crown in Rotterdam, elevating 124 kg in the press and 146 kg in the jerk. This was his best achievement and he remained identified as the *Europameister*, the European champion, throughout his career.

In 1904, Maier progressed decisively and became one of the stars of Central European weightlifting. He began a stiff duel with another of Munich's idols, Alois Selos, for the leadership in Germany and the challenge to the Austrians. The weightlifting experts saw the two lifters as the heirs of the German champion Hans Beck, and their careers crossed paths frequently. The two men became friends over the rivalry, and each invited the other to the premises of his facility for training or for official attempts. The opposite of Selos, who specialised

> THIS WAS HIS BEST ACHIEVEMENT AND HE REMAINED IDENTIFIED AS THE *EUROPAMEISTER*, THE EUROPEAN CHAMPION, THROUGHOUT HIS CAREER.

almost exclusively in two-hands exercises, Maier, a self-trained lifter, cultivated a variety of tests of strength, revealing a greater potential. Among his records is pressing two 50-kg ring weights with two hands 12 times in succession. In the two-hands snatch, his best was 97.5 kg.

In 1905, Maier placed third in the European championships of Amsterdam, pressing 110 kg and jerking 137 kg. That year a case of tendonitis disturbed Maier for a long time as he was approaching his best years. Regardless, he was able to put to the chest with two moves 170 kg and to clean with one move 130 kg. In October, he equalled Beck's former German record in the two-hands jerk—157.5 kg—but Selos had since improved that performance. By the way, in 1904, Maier got overhead 158.375 kg, which would have been the national record, but he was unable to fix the bar for the required five seconds. This attempt was his closest to overtaking the record in that exercise.

In 1906, Selos jerked 162.6 kg, with Maier right behind him exceeding 160 kg. However, if Maier was continuing to improve his personal record in the two-hands continental jerk a bit behind Selos, he excelled in other exercises. He could snatch 80 kg with his right hand, and jerk 90 kg with one hand in the German style, after cleaning it with two hands. He cleaned and pressed, with a slow backbend, 118 kg—a worthwhile performance. In the bent press, he could press 111 kg with his right hand and 108 kg with his left.

In 1907 Maier reached his personal best in the two-hands jerk with 165 kg, only 0.75 kg less than Selos's national record. But on 16 November, just few days after the Parisian performance of the professional Swede Arvid Andersson, who cleaned and jerked the world record of 149 kg, Maier established the German record in the two-hands clean and jerk of 141 kg, better than the French champions like Vasseur and Maspoli and, as an amateur, less than only Scuri's performance. In the same session, with the continental style, he exceeded 151 kg, failing his attempt with 161 kg.

> MAIER WAS ONE SUCH GREAT EXAMPLE—FOR HIS DEDICATION AND HIS WARM HUMAN RELATIONS.

After 1908, with his full attention on his job, Maier returned to competition in 1909 but did not exceed 160 kg anymore. He decided to practise weightlifting for his pleasure only and to offer his skill in fostering younger generations. In Munich, the talent for weightlifting abounded. Maier was one such great example—for his dedication and his warm human relations.

In 1919, after the war, the German federation called the older champions for the moral reconstruction of sport and for motivating the new generations. The federation organised a championships for veterans, and Maier—44 years old at the time and a member of the Munich club Armin—won, being able again to exceed 112.5 kg in the two-hands jerk and 60 kg in the one-hand clean and jerk. He died probably in the 1960s. M

Canada World Strength Presents Fortissimus 2009:

Building on the Tradition of Louis Cyr

William Crawford, M.D.

Louis Cyr continues to stand as a collective ideal of strength among strength purists. As the ancestral home of Cyr, Quebec pays tribute to her strongman in the 2009 Fortissimus.

Although primarily inspired by Louis Cyr, this contest holds many other men in esteem, with events and implements bearing the names of Anderson, Sigmarsson, Dinnie, Kazmaier, and Apollon, to name a few. The implements are carefully chosen in form and crafted in a way that shows them off as objects of beauty to strength enthusiasts like me.

Most importantly, to uphold the reputation of Cyr, Fortissimus is billed as heavier and more challenging than any other strongman event held in the world. The challenge comes not just from adding weight, but by deceptively hiding it in the details of each event, evoking the spirits of the lost disciplines of past great strongmen.

The weekend of 26–28 June 2009 found Montmagny, Quebec invaded by the strongest men in the world to battle for the title of *l'homme le plus fort de la planète*—the strongest man on the planet.

Rolling Thunder® World Championships

What better way to kick off the weekend than to have an IronMind Rolling Thunder World Championships on Friday evening, the night before the competition officially began.

Mark Felix has rewritten the record book as the first man in history to lift over 300 lb. on the Rolling Thunder under authenticated conditions, and the King of the Rolling Thunder came to add another jewel to his crown. Mark told me before the competition that he had lifted 304 lb. in training and was looking for a huge lift.

The competition was held in front of a crowd of several hundred enthusiastic onlookers, with Magnus ver Magnusson serving as the head judge. The principal competitors were Mark Felix, Phil Pfister, Odd Haugen, and Andrus Murumets. Andrus pushed Mark up to

Randall J. Strossen photos.

Andrus Murumets is one of three men in the world who have held the world record in the Rolling Thunder and officially closed the No. 3 Captains of Crush Gripper, so it was an honor to see him back in his first Rolling Thunder competition since 2003.

Phil Pfister (l.) and Odd Haugen (r.) were part of the illustrious field competing in the 2009 Rolling Thunder World Championships.

a 265-lb. lift; however, Mark won the competition with a huge 271-lb. and promptly moved up to a world record weight of 302 lb. Mark made several heroic attempts with this record poundage but ultimately did not make a successful lift. He seemed disappointed with his efforts, but we were thrilled to see a man who owns forearms and hands that belong in the rarified air of Mount Grip Olympus ply his trade in a concerted manner.

116 MILO | Dec. 2009, Vol. 17, No. 3

Mark Felix is the 2009 Rolling Thunder world champion and he has a unique trophy to prove it.

Having secured the world championships title, Mark Felix attacked 302-lb. in a valiant effort, but the lift was not to be.

I said a brief hello to the athletes just after the Rolling Thunder competition. Each man I approached was in a mental state of intense anticipation, all here to wage an epic battle against Earth's attraction to mass.

Day one

The first day of competition started with the Pyramid of Strength (power stairs), which set the tone for the competition—heavy and furious. The implements were 450, 500, and 525 lb., with each consecutive weight to be carried up the 5 stairs. Brian Shaw and Derek Poundstone got the event off to a good start, with Derek edging out Brian. Zydrunas Savickas wanted to lay a firm grip on an early lead and blasted through the event, making 15 stairs in 42 seconds. This result by Zydrunas was 8 seconds ahead of the second-best time set by Misha Koklyaev.

The second event of day one was a 925-lb. Super Yoke, a massive implement with two wooden barrels affixed by a cross bar. Terry Hollands posted a daunting time of 19.4 seconds over the 30-m course in the second pairing of the event. His time held until the final pairing of Zydrunas and Misha. Both started strongly, but Misha faltered.

Zydrunas Savickas might have been able to beat the forklift in a race down the course.

© RANDALL J. STROSSEN, PH.D.

Two events into the contest, after the Super Yoke, Derek Poundstone was four points behind Zydrunas Savickas.

Zydrunas moved briskly through the first 15 m, and then amazingly he accelerated through the last half of the race! Zydrunas finished in 18 seconds and set a new world record.

Erik Sauve made the trip with me and both of us laughed in dis-belief, watching Zydrunas pick up that kind of speed at the end of the race.

The third event was the Sigmarsson Wheels Deadlift, an iconic-looking apparatus that weighs 880 lb., with the bar set at 17-1/2" from the floor, with competitors using straps. With this type of prodigious back strength in the competition, we were in for some serious pulling. Jimmy Marku started off the event with 9 repetitions. Shortly thereafter, Mark Felix locked onto the bar and garnered 13 reps. Mark is pure pulling power in motion when you watch him deadlift—no leverage needed, just fantastic back and hip strength. Zydrunas was second with 11 reps, and Poundstone came in third with 10 reps.

The much anticipated IronMind Overhead World Challenge was the fourth event of the day. Five implements were used, for a total of 1,893 lb. In order, they were: 1) the 1980 log at 346.5 lb.; 2) the 1892 Apollon axle at 366 lb.; 3) the 1988 Kazmaier log at 375 lb.; 4) the IronMind Apollon's Axle at 390 lb.; and 5) the 2004 Z log at 415 lb. Several athletes lifted the first two implements, with Travis Ortmayer the first among them in 20.9 seconds, and Andrus Murumets following in 21.8 seconds. Then came Zydrunas. He nailed the first implement easily. While lifting the 366-lb. axle, Zydrunas stumbled forward but was able to press it—strength that almost mocked this stalwart implement. The 375-lb. log was pressed in short order, in a time of 29.3 seconds. Zydrunas cleaned the 390-lb. axle, sending the crowd into a roar, but with a somewhat awkward

Brian Shaw settles in with the log, one element in the IronMind Overhead World Challenge.

rack he returned the implement to the platform without attempting a press. Zydrunas presses in the strictest manner—no knee bend, no hip bend, and no leaning back.

The Slater King of Stones World Challenge was the fifth and final event of an epic first day. Six Slater Atlas Stones, weighing from 300 to 425 in 25-lb. increments, were used. The boxes started at 68" high and decreased to 50" high in 4" decrements. Zydrunas showed his only glimpse of mortality this day with a sixth-place finish, lifting 5 stones in 44.9 seconds. But this was sixth place by .1 seconds behind Misha and 1.2 seconds behind Andrus. Poundstone showed his usual consistency and placed third, with 2006 World's Strongest Man winner Phil Pfister in the hunt with a strong second-place finish of 29.5 seconds. Brian Shaw put in a terrific performance and won the event by being the only man to lift the 425-lb. stone onto the 50" box. Brian is an enormous man, for sure. I had my picture taken with him outside the arena—my wife commented that he didn't look that tall but I had to remind her I was standing on the street curb!

At the end of the first day the top places were as follows: 1. Savickas, 64 points; 2. Poundstone, 58; 3. Shaw, 52.5; 4. Ortmayer, 49; and 5) Koklyaev, 43.

I had asked Zydrunas at the end of the day if he had skipped competition for 7 months, including the Arnold Classic, just to rest and prepare for this competition. If you recall, he was defeated by Poundstone the year before in the final event on the final lift with the historic Cyr stone. Zydrunas looked over his shoulder at me, wryly smiled, and said, "I prepare for every competition." I took that as a diplomatic and understated yes to my question. With Derek breathing down his neck, the next day was shaping up to be just what the lusty throngs in attendance had come to see in Montmagny—a rematch between Zydrunas and Derek for supremacy.

Day two

The first event of the second day was the Inukshuk/Husafell Medley Challenge. The medley started with a carry-and-load, in which 4 barrels of increasing weight—225, 250, 275, and 300 lb.—were carried 7.5 m and loaded onto a chest-high platform. Next up was loading 2 barrels—400 and 425 lb.—onto short platforms, followed by carrying a 400-lb. steel replica Husafell Stone over a 20-m course. The final leg required the competitors to load the steel replica Inukshuk Stone (Inuit manhood stone) weighing 425 lb. This was a challenge that required strength, endurance, and grit.

He'd already made his mark on the strongman world, but Fortissimus underlined the ascendency of Brian Shaw, the only man to load the sixth and final Atlas Stone.

Terry Hollands was the seventh strongman to take the challenge and the first to complete the entire medley, in which he had a particularly impressive carry with the Husafell replica. Zydrunas was the next athlete to complete the medley, with a 20-second improvement in time. Poundstone finished in a scorching time of 59 seconds, a full 9 seconds faster than Zydrunas. Brian Shaw was the last athlete of the event and had an excellent time of 69 seconds, only 1 second behind Zydrunas. Derek had a resounding win, with Zydrunas and Brian in second and third. The theme of the competition continued to play itself out and almost to a T.

> THE THEME OF THE COMPETITION CONTINUED TO PLAY ITSELF OUT AND ALMOST TO A T.

Derek Poundstone, who's a cop, knows what a well-placed knee can do, and he applied the same principle to win the Inukshuk stone's cooperation.

Flanked by Ekaterina Mayorskaya (l.), and Dione Wessels (r.), Marcel Mostert (c.) takes a look at the scores.

Jimmy Marku flies on the keg loading.

Just a comment on the Inukshuk/Husafell Medley. Some may say that a steel implement does not equal the Husafell Stone. However, as someone who has a fondness for the Husafell Stone, I find the metal replica a fine tribute to Iceland's icon.

The second event of day two was called a hip and thigh back lift, and it was more like a partial squat that was set up so that you could also use your arms. The weight started at 2,000 lb. (908 kg) and increased by 250 lb. to the last man standing. To eliminate a height disadvantage for the taller athletes, the apparatus was set at predetermined heights so that each lifter completed the same lift.

The first round at 2,000 lb. was fairly uneventful, with a highlight of Phil Pfister standing completely as if squatting the weight. Five athletes completed a lift with 2,500 lb., including Louis-Philippe Jean, Ortmayer, Shaw, Savickas, and Poundstone. The weight climbed and Louis-Philippe electrified the crowd with a lift of 2,750 lb.

Louis-Philippe Jean, a local hero, tied with Zydrunas Savickas on this lift that was called a "hip and thigh back lift," but had the mechanics of a partial squat.

Zydrunas actually held his body upright to lift 2,750 lb.—as if squatting—instead of bending forward to utilize a greater leverage advantage. Truly impressive. In the end, Zydrunas and Louis-Philippe tied for first.

The third event of the grueling second day was the Louis Cyr Dumbbell Power Walk. The event featured two pairs of beautiful, solid-cast, long-handled dumbbells—the first pair weighing 325 lb. each and the second pair weighing 352 lb. each. The challenge was to power walk 30 m with the first pair and return 30 m with the second and heavier pair. Poundstone won the event with a time of 38 seconds. Following closely were Murumets, Felix, and Pfister in that order. The bigger story in this event is that Zydrunas did not finish the second half, putting him in ninth place. At the end of this event, Poundstone led overall by a half point over Zydrunas—a very surprising turn of events in the face of such a dominating performance by Savickas up to this point.

Again, another set of beautiful implements was highlighted in the fourth event of the day. Seven single-cast dumbbells were to be cleaned and pressed overhead with one hand each, starting with 150-lb. for both the left and right hands; and followed by one-hand lifts with 175, 195, 205, 215 and finally 225 lb. Most of the athletes actually snatched the 150-lb. dumbbell with each hand. Six athletes completed the first 6 dumbbells, separated only by time for placement, with Murumets first among them. Ortmayer claimed second place by completing all 7

Andrus Murumets at speed on the Farmer's Walk.

Travis Ortmayer was the only man other than Zydrunas Savickas to succeed on all seven dumbbells, the second stage in the IronMind Overhead World Challenge.

required lifts, with terrific form on the last implement. As a pressing event, however, you know where this is going: Zydrunas lifted all 7—including the tremendous 225-lb. dumbbell—in strict style and all in 18.5 seconds. Cyr was smiling somewhere, I am sure.

With Zydrunas regaining the lead on the ninth event, a familiar scenario unfolded. The tenth and last event was the Slater King of Stones Challenge. The competitors were to lift four natural stones, including the now famous Cyr/Poundstone stone weighing 530 lb., onto platforms. In order, the stones weighed 350, 400, 450, and 530 lb.

The memories of Fortissimus 2008 weighed heavily in the air as the athletes went down to the stones to size them up. Poundstone and Savickas were conspicuously absent from this group, as if using this time to summon the strength gods and cash in on their sweat equity at this pivotal moment.

Shaw was third in the final event with three stones in 31.8 seconds. Poundstone was second with 30.2 seconds, including a terrific effort with the Cyr/Poundstone stone. Zydrunas finished strongly, completing the competition as the victor, with a winning time of 18.5 seconds and three stones lifted. He was not to be denied this year.

The final overall scores for the top three were:

1. Zydrunas Savickas   124.5 points
2. Derek Poundstone   118
3. Brian Shaw   106.5

Also, the Big Z won the IronMind Overhead World Challenge by virtue of his performances with the pressing events, and Brian Shaw won the Slater King of Stones Challenge.

As the historian Martin van Creveld stated regarding military campaigns, "Amateurs study tactics and professionals study logistics." As someone who organizes a large strength event myself (athletics for the New Hampshire Highland Games), I marveled at the tremendous field of athletes, the beautiful implements, and the precision timing of running the events. No doubt someone was watching them from afar . . . Louis Cyr himself. **M**

Relaxed, friendly, and embodying the relentless power of a tractor, Zydrunas Savickas added another title to his most impressive collection.

Grassroots to Gold Medals:
Play Your Role

Paul Doherty   Coach, Sacramento High School

In my two previous articles I discussed in broad terms our approach at Hassle Free to developing a solid weightlifting program aimed at junior-level athletes. The main points made were the focus on recruitment and basic-level programming that would allow for top-level athletes to climb the ranks very quickly, giving them opportunities not found elsewhere, in an effort to funnel the best we can find into the weightlifting pipeline in the U.S.

I am no ignorant fool and clearly recognize the lack of talent and depth here in the U.S. and have heard far too often the cries of mediocrity echoing from our membership. I have presented clear examples of foreign programs that so far exceed our limits that catching up seems not just improbable, but hopeless. My humble thoughts here again can only speak to the experiences we have had at Sacramento High in an effort to close those gaps and gain that ground we have so disturbingly lost.

At the 2009 School-Age Nationals, USAW director of high performance Mike Gattone hosted a coaches' seminar and group discussion on some of these very points. In this article I'd like to make reference to those points and shed some light on what some of us are doing to address them.

Paul Fleschler, the former head men's resident coach in Colorado Springs and current coach at the time, made some emotional comments to the small congregation. In summary, he had just felt personal embarrassment at the performances of our men's team at the Pan-Am Games just a few weeks prior. He spoke vividly of the toughness, competitiveness, and dynamic spirit of the other Pan-American lifters and countries. He passionately expressed his discouragement at the lack of such performances from the U.S. lifters. The precision and athleticism of lifts executed by the Pan-American countries were impressive to say the least, with downright gutsy and clutch performances, to give credit to their emotions. The bronze medals won by 94-kg lifter Norik Vardanian and +105-lifter Patrick Judge were the only two won by the U.S. men, who in even recent years have come home with more.

Many members of the weightlifting world thought I was crazy when they heard that not one but two of our top Hassle Free athletes, Donavan Ford (2009 105-kg junior national champion and junior world top-place finisher) and Keylin Mackey (second-place finisher in the 85-kg class at the junior nationals), were being encouraged to continue their training in Colorado Springs. The arguments came pouring down about how well they had done under our supervision and about how much they meant to our program locally. We were warned about all of the failed athletes who had crumbled in Colorado, and we were urged to reconsider. This was the wave of support I received from within USAW, and it goes to show the disconnect within our own organization and probable causes of our failed progress.

I am sending my athletes to the Olympic Training Center, and the reaction I received was one of aghast opposition. I tried to remind these concerned constituents that Donavan and Keylin have done well for two reasons. First, they are tremendous athletes, recruited because of what they have accomplished and what they will continue to conquer. Second, they are products of what we like to refer to as a weightlifting factory. Our coaching prowess falls far too short of the highly technical and highly specific adjustments they need to make under intense supervision. We cannot allocate enough time to such details. We are fulfilling our role in the pipeline that should be USA Weightlifting. We mass recruit and promote, and then send off the select few to a better place.

It goes without saying that the OTC is not the place for everyone, and that many, if not most, of our top international performances have come from athletes who opt to train at home. However, the provision of ample food, comfortable housing, and accessible sports medicine at the OTC cannot be disputed. There is no excuse for failed weightlifters there, and the programming and coaching they receive is top-caliber. Those qualities made Colorado Springs an attractive option for our two fortunate athletes, and we expect nothing but top results from each of them. However, it is not the only path, and we have even proven it here at Hassle Free.

As we close in on 2010, we will take the national stage, competing at the senior level for the very first time. Although our team is still comprised mostly of junior-level lifters, a few of our first athletes have finally grown to the ripe young age of 21 and will no longer dominate the junior division but take their swings at the seniors. One such athlete is UC Davis junior David Garcia.

David was one of our most accomplished weightlifters throughout his high school years, winning one School-Age and one Junior National Championships. Furthermore, David was also one of the nation's top students and earned acceptance at one of California's top academic institutions to pursue a degree in biochemistry. He was sidelined by a torn labrum in his shoulder that derailed a near lock on the Junior World Team in 2009, but he will be back in 2010 one year older.

He and Donavan both will be medal winners at the senior level in 2010, and while Donavan is taking his sets under the close watch of resident coaches in Colorado, the best fit for David now is to continue training locally.

My point in this article is simply this: regardless of where our athletes train, they are OUR athletes, as in Team USA. Too many egos in the sport who are concerned about who gets what credit for what performance will

> WE WERE WARNED ABOUT ALL OF THE FAILED ATHLETES WHO HAD CRUMBLED IN COLORADO, AND WE WERE URGED TO RECONSIDER.

> ... REGARDLESS OF WHERE OUR ATHLETES TRAIN, THEY ARE OUR ATHLETES, AS IN TEAM USA.

only slow our athletes' progress. While we sit and bicker over such trivial matters, the Germans are squatting. This truth never hit me as forcefully as it did in that conference room at the School-Age Nationals. Paul Fleschler and Dennis Snethen, among others, hit the nail right on the head: we need to stop whining and start lifting. Check your ego at the door, do what's best for your (our) athlete, and work together to produce better results.

One of the best and newest weightlifting coaches in the country is one of our colleagues, Robert Earwicker. Rob was a competitive lifter for many years in the U.K. and would laugh if I listed his many accomplishments here in MILO. This is because his head isn't full of hot air—it's just right in size where, as Jim Schmitz would say, his legs are strong enough to hold it. He currently coaches a few up-and-coming lifters, but unfortunately, like many of our members out there, works in a gym where he doesn't have access to the nation's top talent. Regardless, he doesn't sit idly by on the sidelines to watch my brother Kevin and me run frantic with 100 athletes at a local meet. He gets up and joins the assault by offering any guidance he can to our top lifters. It is easier and more efficient for him to work with our polished athletes while Kevin and I organize the chaos of first-time lifters. This doesn't bother me one bit. And never for one second would Rob try to take credit for coaching the biggest clean and jerk at the PWA Junior Championships. The point is, we work together to produce the best possible totals.

Furthermore, working at a private facility, Rob has worked diligently with Dave Corbin to organize and host some of the best local events in the country. Their professional approach has contributed to a real element lacking across the nation. Their top-notch venue and events provide legitimacy to our sport that we cannot provide our own athletes.

> QUIT POINTING FINGERS AND PASSING BLAME. SUPPORT OUR ATHLETES AND THEIR COACHES ANY WAY YOU CAN.

After hearing those arguments from our membership, I would encourage everyone to play his or her role in closing the gap that at least all of us can agree exists. Quit pointing fingers and passing blame. Support our athletes and their coaches any way you can. Instead of bashing other missteps by U.S. lifters in order to make yourself feel better, step up to the plate and do your part. Kevin and I have 100% confidence that we are doing everything we can to play our role in recruiting athletes. Now, it is up to the staff at the OTC to develop and mature that talent. Maybe you don't have any athletes under your direct supervision right now—that's okay. Go to a local meet and volunteer your time and expertise. Be a fan! Cheer, buy a t-shirt. Look at the sports around us that produce world-class performances from these same athletes and start filling in the gaps.

London 2012 is closer than people think, and if you bicker for even just one second longer, you'll have plenty more to crab about as our sport loses even more ground. Step up to the plate and get it done; or as we like to say here at Hassle Free for 2009, "Put it on the bar!" Contribute in any way you can.

M

The Iron Mine

Equipment

Atlas Stone Molds from Slater's!
Easy to make, hard to break, heavy-duty poly-Lexan, for time-after-time uses in 8, 10, 12, 14, 16, 18, 20, & 24-inch dia. Low int'l & dom. S&H. 740-654-2204. E-mail steve@slatershardware.com; dealers: www.slatershardware.com, www.totalperformancesports.com, www.marunde-muscle.com, www.prowriststraps.com.

IronMind Goods in Germany!
Books, gear, equipment and MORE! www.c-of-c.de, Choice of Champions, Dr. Hermann Korte, Recklinghaeuser Str. 119, 45721 Haltern am See, Germany; e-mail info@k3k.de.

Strength Equipment
from the FIRST to close the No. 3 Captains of Crush Gripper. Custom super-duty racks, benches and selectorized machines by Sorinex. Owned, designed and tested to be virtually bombproof by Richard Sorin. 16 years of experience supplying universities, gyms and serious lifters nationwide. Call and talk with The Grip Man at 877-767-4639, P.O. Box 121, Irmo, SC 29063; visit our website at www.sorinex.com and see our training tips section!

Real Wood Strongman Logs
Slater's True Logs are built to last, used in top pro strongman contests. E-mail steve@slatershardware.com, 740-654-2204; www.slatershardware.com.

CoC Key: From Miles to Mils
Trim that gap (between the handles of your Captains of Crush Grippers) and then make it disappear! The CoC Key will help you unlock your next rounds of PRs, giving you a precise way to gauge your progress. How big was that gap, really? With steps of 2, 4, 6, 8, 10, 12, 14 and 16 mm, the CoC Key will tell you exactly where you are . . . which is the first step to getting where you'd rather be. $9.95 + S&H: $4 USA, US$7 Canada, US$13 all others. Visit our on-line store at www.ironmind.com.

Equipment

Strength Equipment/Stone Molds
Nothing but the best strength training/ strongman equipment: harnesses, stone molds, kettlebells, books, DVDs and more. www.totalperformancesports.com. 617-387-5998.

World-class VULKAN Supports
Heavy-duty, high-quality: knee, arm, back, & pants for strongman, powerlifters, heavy events, bodybuilders. Retail & wholesale. www.theweakgeteaten.com.

Free Catalog: IronMind Enterprises Tools of the Trade for Serious Strength Athletes
IronMind is the home of Captains of Crush® Grippers, *SUPER SQUATS*, Just Protein®, *MILO*®, the Vulcan Racks II+ System Squat Racks, Strong-Enough Lifting Straps™, and the Draft Horse Pulling Harness™, not to mention the world's leading line of grip tools, a top-quality line of gym equipment, strongman training equipment for the world's strongest men, and books, posters, and DVDs to inform and inspire you to greater success. While we sell plenty of equipment to champion strength athletes around the world, our specialty is the dedicated home trainer—strong guys who train in their garages, basements and backyards. Take a look at what we have to offer. P.O. Box 1228, Nevada City, CA 95959 USA; t - 530-272-3579; f – 530-272-3095; website and on-line store: www.ironmind.com; e-mail: sales@ironmind.com.

Strong, Pain-Free Hands
In one convenient package: now **three** vital training tools and guide for preventing, reducing, or eliminating hand pain. Kit includes IronMind EGG, Expand-Your-Hand Bands, Wrist-Relief Soft Weight, and booklet "How to Develop Strong, Pain-Free Hands." $51.85 + S&H: $12 USA, US$18 Canada, US$35 all others. Available in our on-line store at www.ironmind.com, or send payment to IronMind Enterprises, Inc., P.O. Box 1228, Nevada City, CA 95959 USA.

Websites, Training Forums

The IronMind News
The Strength World's News Source. Fast. Accurate. Objective. www.ironmind.com.

Captains of Crush Grippers Fans
The facts, fiction, myths about Captains of Crush Grippers: training programs, history highlights, gripper glossary, how-tos & FAQs—it's all here. www.captainsofcrushgrippers.com.

Sustain Strength & Speed
Battling Ropes: you read about them in *MILO*. Learn more John Brookfield's strength and conditioning system at www.battlingropes.com.

PrimordialStrengthSystems.com
Creating the most explosive athletes through the science of persistence.

Strong and Healthy Hands for Everyone
www.strongandhealthyhands.com.

Strengthcoach.tv
For trainees and coaches—advancing the fundamental, creative, and limitless potential of strength development methodology.

Training: Magazines, Books, DVDs

Free Illustrated Catalog!
Books, courses, back-date magazines, out-of-prints, new, etc. Classic how-to training methods and biographies by all the old masters. Buy, sell, trade, collecting over 25 years. Bill Hinbern, 32430-E Cloverdale, Farmington, MI 48336; www.superstrengthbooks.com.

Real Strength Real Muscle
This article anthology by the late Coach John Christy is for Real People with Real Lives: those who want to get bigger, stronger, and better conditioned without sacrificing family, school, or work. Real routines, real trainees, real answers, real nutritional guidance. 408 pp. $46.50 ppd. USA / US$71.50 ppd. others. DVDs also available. Order from www.realstrengthrealmuscle.com/book.htm.

MILO | Dec. 2009, Vol. 17, No. 3   127

The Iron Mine

Training: Magazines, Books, DVDs

The Steel Tip Newsletter by Dr. Ken is once again available. www.oldetime-strongman.com. 1-800-978-0206.

Updated! Captains of Crush Grippers book
Whether you want to get an A+ on your next gripper exam or only care about building a stronger grip, you'll want to get this book—now updated and expanded to include over 20% new material, and most of it on training. Dedicated to all who know "it's not a crush . . . it's an obsession!" 192 pp. $19.95 + S&H $5.00 USA, US$7.00 Can., US$13.00 all others. IronMind Enterprises, www.ironmind.com.

Powerlifting USA
Contest results, schedules, training. 12 iss/year; $36.95 US; $96.00 elsewhere. PLUSA, P. O. Box 467, Camarillo, CA 93011.

Paul Anderson's Books and Tapes
The Paul Anderson Youth Home offers a free catalog of Paul's books and tapes, as well as the Coleman video on Paul's life. This gives you a unique opportunity to learn from the world's strongest man while helping to support the youth home which Paul Anderson was dedicated to building. For a copy of this catalog, contact: Paul Anderson Youth Home, P. O. Box 525, Vidalia, GA 30475, e-mail: info@payh.org.

The Get-Big-and-Strong Program
SUPER SQUATS: How to Gain 30 Pounds of Muscle in 6 Weeks: this is the program that has turned human toothpicks into stalwarts and stalwarts into legends. After a few minutes under a squat bar, you will find out what you're made of; and if you want to get bigger and stronger and have no use for drugs, fancy equipment, or the latest food supplement fad, this is your book. 112 pp. $16.95 plus S&H: $5/US; $7/Can; $13/all others; www.ironmind.com.

Steve Justa's "High Plains Heavy Metal IronMaster's Bible"
No bull, strength-building tips. 300 big pages, big lifts, big poses, over 40 photos. Send $20.00 to Steve Justa, Box 97, Harvard, NE 68944.

Training: Magazines, Books, DVDs

Be Your Best by David Morgan
Crosstraining for CrossFit's King Kong? Author and Olympian weightlifter Morgan smashed the CrossFit King Kong record in his first attempt—and with 275/500 instead of 250/455 in the clean and DL. Want to be strong and fit? You'll want his book on training to be your best. 128 pp. $19.95 + S&H: $7.00 USA/US$10.00 Can/US$16.00 other. www.ironmind.com.

Weightlifting Videos
20 high-quality DVDs from every weight class of the 2006 USA W/L Nat. Jr. Champs & Pan-Am Qualifier, $30/session; e-mail WeightliftingVideoDirect@gmail.com for compressed samples or to order.

Denis Reno's Newsletter
The quickest and best way to get Olympic weightlifting results, from local contests to World Championships. $26/year US, $30 Can., $45–$50 others. Denis Reno, 30 Cambria Road, Newton, MA 02165; e-mail: renoswlnl@verizon.net.

NEW! Battling Ropes DVD
Featuring Ingrid Marcum, champion weightlifter and Olympic bobsled team hopeful, this DVD shows you how to build strength and stamina using the unique Battling Ropes system developed by John Brookfield. Aimed at both individuals and teams, the system uses a long, heavy rope to train at high levels of intensity for longer durations, increasing your ability to generate and sustain power. Strongmen, football players, Special Forces types especially, you'll want this. 48 min., NTSC. $39.95 plus S&H: $4/US; $7/Can; $13/all others; www.ironmind.com.

Defying Gravity
by Bill Starr. Signed. Hard cover $20, soft cover $15 + $4.00 S&H. Bill Starr, 1011 Warwick Drive, #3-C, Aberdeen, MD 21001.

Starr Novel
The Susquehanna River Hills Chronicles, a novel by Bill Starr. $20 + $6 S&H USA; 1011 Warwick Drive, #3-C, Aberdeen, MD 21001.

Training: Magazines, Books, DVDs

World Weightlifting
The official magazine of the International Weightlifting Federation; its four issues a year cover contests worldwide. $40/year Europe, $50 elsewhere. World Weightlifting, IWF Secretariat, 1146 Budapest, Istvanmezei ut 1-3, Hungary.

Associations

The Association of Oldetime Barbell & Strongmen
A not-to-be-missed annual reunion and dinner—next year, it's on October 23, 2010—for some of the biggest names in the Iron Game. Members receive a very interesting newsletter. Annual donation is $25, payable to AOBS, c/o Artie Drechsler, President, 33-30 – 150 Street, Flushing, NY 11354; email: lifttech@earthlink.net; www.wlinfo.com.

Join USA Weightlifting!
The National Governing Body for the Olympic sport. Go to www.usaweightlifting.org or call 719-866-4508, for news about recent competitions and courses, membership information, local and national events, coaching education, and the newest items available on-line. Membership benefits include participant accident insurance, a subscription to *Weightlifting, USA,* and **super discounts** on airline tickets, hotels, car rentals, and other products and services through our Olympic partnership!

The Iron Mine

Looking to buy or sell? Want to give your upcoming contest an extra boost? Advertise in the Iron Mine. $10 per line per insertion, no minimum number of lines. No display ads, please. All material subject to approval. Send advertising copy or direct questions to: *MILO*, P.O. Box 1228, Nevada City, CA 95959, tel 530-272-3579, fax 530-272-3095, sales@ironmind.com. *We try to screen the advertising, but let the buyer beware.*